D0248631

LONDON BOROUGH OF BARNET

The **CRUMBS** Family Cookbook

The CRUMBS Family Cookbook

150 REALLY QUICK & VERY EASY RECIPES

CLAIRE AND LUCY MCDONALD
AWARD-WINNING FAMILY FOOD BLOGGERS

CICO BOOKS
LONDON NEW YORK

Published in 2014 by CICO Books
an imprint of Ryland Peters & Small
519 Broadway, 5th floor, New York NY 10012
20–21 Jockey's Fields, London WC1R 4BW

www.rylandpeters.com

10 9 8 7 6 5 4 3 2 1

Text copyright © Claire McDonald and Lucy McDonald 2014
Design and photographs copyright © CICO Books 2014

The authors' moral rights have been asserted. All rights reserved.
No part of this publication may be reproduced, stored in a retrieval
system, or transmitted in any form or by any means, electronic,
mechanical, photocopying, or otherwise, without the prior
permission of the publisher.

A CIP catalogue record for this book is available from the Library
of Congress and the British Library.

UK ISBN 978 1 78249 155 2
US ISBN 978 1 78249 172 9

Printed in China

Project Editor: Gillian Haslam
Photographer: Stuart West
Home Economist: Emily Jonzen
Food Stylist: Luis Peral Ananda
Design: Mark Latter
Copy Editor: Lee Faber
Illustrations: Hannah George

To Our Mum
Thank you

CONTENTS

INTRODUCTION

Welcome. Since you had children has cooking changed? Rather than dinners à deux, glass of wine in hand, do you spend evenings chiselling porridge off the walls? Yes? Then welcome to our world.

We are two sisters who like cooking and love eating. Pre-kids, food had been fun. We had enjoyed reading cookery books and cutting complicated recipes out of the Sunday papers. Sometimes we even made them. But then we had kids and were suddenly knocking together four meals a day – breakfast, lunch, their dinner and our dinner. There were only a few minutes in the day when we weren't cooking. Or washing up. From being our greatest comforter, food had somehow turned into the harshest of taskmasters.

There was only one thing for it – a private chef. Back in the real world we realised that if we were going to get on top of the situation, it would need a concerted effort from both of us. Lucy already had her killer Coconut Macaroon recipe (see page 150) – great to make with kids, but also a miraculous hangover cure when served with a double espresso. Claire had a Broccoli Pasta (see page 43) dish that was quick to make, delectable to eat and had made some of her mummy friends sob with gratitude when she shared the recipe with them.

But we knew we'd need more than two recipes to keep us going over the next 18 years of parenting. So we started a family food blog (www.crumbsfood.co.uk) and YouTube channel (www.youtube.com/crumbsfood) to help inspire us.

We started baking, braising, basting, whisking, whipping and weighing. Every meal our families enjoyed we noted down on the blog. But these weren't any old recipes. Nope! These were fast. These were easy. These were tasty and, most importantly, could be done while keeping an eye on the children/supervising homework/ cooling forehead on kitchen floor (delete as appropriate). We prided ourselves on cooking recipes that gave a two-breadstick salute to long ingredients lists and said *hello!* to the culinary shortcut. They suited the fast pace of family life.

And do you know what? We discovered we were not alone. Despite there being loads of celebrity chefs, recipe books and food blogs out there, quite a few people liked ours. They felt that what we were saying reflected how they felt. They (you?) were also looking for recipes for real families, where the fridge was often empty and good intentions were often thwarted by a hard day at the parenting coalface.

This sense of camaraderie, of knackered parents reaching out across the ether, made so much of our daily grind worth it. We stopped begrudging all that time we'd spent on our knees chasing peas under the dining table. We no longer wanted a private chef.

And then we got asked to write this book – woo hoo! Icing, meet cake. In it we've included a few of our blog's big hitters. We hesitate to say our Broccoli Pasta (see page 43) has been a YouTube sensation, but, well, it's true. The Fairy Castle Cake in the Celebrate chapter (see page 174) is similarly famous. But we've also come up with oodles of recipes never seen on the blog or our YouTube channel. We hope you will like them.

How to use this book

We have grouped each chapter by theme, but go to pages 10–11 for an alternative index. We've got recipes in under 5 minutes and 10 minutes, plus meals which are perfect for playdates. Do midweek suppers for you and your partner normally pass in a haze of exhaustion? We've got some great grown-up suggestions that you can knock up quickly and healthily. Is the cupboard bare? Our selection of store cupboard staples on page 8, alongside our store cupboard recipes (listed on page 10–11) means you will never go hungry again. Without wanting to boast, some of our recipes are good enough to serve to friends. We are not suggesting you serve our Hipster chilli (see page 60) as part of an eight course feast, but if some local friends are popping round, it's a nice easy thing to make.

We've also crammed this book with as many helpful hints and tips as possible. Want to know the easiest way to melt chocolate? We give it to you on page 164. In a real hurry and need to cook pasta in double-quick time? Go to page 48 and have your mind blown. Flicking through this book means you might stumble on a tip that could save you valuable time and energy, even if you're not interested in the specific recipe it is attached to.

Who are me?

'We are two sisters with two husbands and four children between us, aged between 4 and 8. We live in opposite corners of London, but wish we lived next door to each other, especially when Claire is baking a Victorian Mess (see page 183). We are not cooks, just women who like to eat.'

Claire 'I like fish, liver and oysters. I'm the Queen of Cobble. I try to buy all ingredients from local shops, with two young children in tow, so the cupboards are frequently bare. Luckily my personal philosophy towards recipe ingredients lists is the shorter the better, so I look at an empty cupboard as a challenge. I'm a journalist, and worked at The Times for over 10 years.'

Lucy 'I like tacos, roast chicken and Coconut Macaroons (see page 150). I try to menu plan but often ruin it all by sneaking in a mid-week Thai takeaway. I have realised that the more organised I am, the better we all eat. That said, all the best laid plans of mice and men…. I'm a journalist too. Newspapers, TV – in fact, whoever will have me.'

' We both like chocolate. And red wine.'

WHAT'S IN OUR CUPBOARDS?

The secret to knocking up great meals in super-quick time is having the right ingredients to hand. This book is full of suggested buys (pre-chopped onions, anyone?). Here are a few more that make cooking just that little bit easier. Some are obvious, others less so.

Store cupboard

Eggs

Capers

Gherkins

Olives

Anchovies

Tinned sardines and tuna

Pine nuts

Tinned tomatoes

Tins of slow-cooked onions fried in olive oil (called Eazy Onions in Britain)

Tins of white beans, butter beans, haricot beans, chickpeas

Puy lentils

Cous cous

Gnocchi

Arborio rice (add odds and ends from the fridge and you have a risotto)

Pasta (normal and fast-cook – ready in 3 minutes)

Ready-cooked noodles

Runny honey

Mustard

Wraps (disparate fridge-dwelling items can become a meal when cut up small and enveloped in a wrap)

Horseradish/mustard/chilli flakes all add a bit of zing at the end of cooking, if you've kept the seasoning down for the children

Extra virgin olive oil

Sesame oil

Soy sauce

Balsalmic and white wine vinegar

Coconut milk

Peanut butter

Stock capsules or cubes

Plain flour

Sugar

Cream crackers

Freezer

Prawns/shrimp

White fish fillets

Fish fingers

Frozen vegetables (peas, green beans, edamame beans, vegetable mixes, sweetcorn and peppers)

Ice cream

Frozen raspberries (great for smoothies or a last minute dessert with vanilla cream and meringue)

Frozen pastry – puff and short crust, ideally all butter

Ready-cooked Yorkshire puddings (shhhhh, we won't tell)

Fridge

Cheese – Parmesan, Cheddar, Mozzarella, Feta and Halloumi

Cream cheese

Smoked salmon (also freezes brilliantly)

Chorizo

Hummus (great emergency lunch)

Ready-chopped onions

Greek yogurt

Crème fraîche

Garlic

White wine, for cooking or drinking

With this lot in your kitchen you'll be able to weather whatever vagaries family life throws at you. With a smile.

Read this!
10 AMAZING CHEATS
which make cooking easier

1. Frozen chopped onions At about the same price as the normal unchopped kind, these babies will cut at least 10 minutes of peeling/chopping/sobbing from your cooking time. Available in bags from the frozen aisle in just about any supermarket. Cooking from scratch just got much easier.

2. Frozen soffrito Have you detected a theme yet? Soffrito is a mix of finely chopped onion, celery and carrot. This Italian holy trinity adds depth to many dishes and is usually the result of some time-consuming and dextrous knife skills. Not any more. Head to the freezer aisle of most supermarkets and a packet of this awaits. One cut (of the packet) is all that is needed.

3. Quick-cook pasta Admittedly normal pasta isn't exactly long-cook, but 11 minutes can seem like an eternity when you've got hungry children baying. A packet of this in the cupboard means a meal is only ever 5 minutes away. Again, find it in your local supermarket with the normal pasta. Cooking time ranges between 3 and 5 minutes.

4. Frozen fruit Admit it, you were already worried your children weren't eating five portions of fruit and veg a day, when experts say we should now eat seven. Never fear, frozen fruit is here. Cheaper than its fresh counterpart, it's available in bags from the freezer aisle (it's like Mecca over there). Bung it in the blender with some juice and yogurt for a fruit smoothie in the morning and one of those portions is ticked off, before you've had breakfast. You don't even need to defrost.

5. Ready-made pastry Pasties, pies, tarts and roll overs. Ready-rolled, ready-made shortcrust and puff pastry can turn the least promising fridge contents into a delectable feast. A few veg, a bit of cheese et voila, a deli-worthy lunch is served.

6. Leftovers It might sound obvious, but make too much of everything. Mashed potato can be transformed into potato bread, stew can become a hearty soup. Once you've cooked something, it just takes a few tweaks to turn it into something else, and you are not having to start from scratch.

7. Wraps The filling is irrelevant if you stick it in a wrap. Chop it up small (you might even get some vegetables in there), smear the wrap with hummus and ta da! Lunch from the random ingredients in your fridge. Add some falafel (see page 77) or golden carrot fritters (see page 127) and you've hit good parenting gold. Turn them into quesadillas (sandwich grated Cheddar cheese between two wraps, fry in butter on each side in a large pan until a gooey mess) and your kids will love you forever.

8. Whipped cream and strawberries These two are the lipstick and push-up bra of the cake world. If your sponge has sunk, your brownies burnt or your Maderia sponge/pound loaf is shop-bought, no one will care if you dress your cake up with a bit of whipped cream and some fresh strawberries.

9. Tinned fish Admittedly tinned fish suffers from an image problem, but it is your friend. If you have a couple of tins of tuna or sardines in your cupboard you will never order takeaway pizza again.

10. Noodles The part-cooked superfast ones are the most brilliant store-cupboard staple. Just add a handful of peas or sweetcorn/corn kernels, some soy sauce, a bit of garlic and supper is less than 3 minutes away. Fast food at its very best.

WHAT TO COOK WHEN

If time is of the essence or your inspiration is at an all-time low, this is your at-a-glance guide to what to cook when.

Meals in 5 minutes

Gnocchi bake (p40)

Sunday night pesto (p46)

Tantrum-averting salmon dill pasta (p48)

Meatballs and spinach (p54)

The thigh's the limit (p57)

Summer bruschetta (p70)

Salmon with artichokes and anchovies (p94)

Cherry tomato tart with mozzarella and basil (p98)

Cheese and Marmite welsh rarebit (p128)

Sardine sandwiches (p131)

Meals in 10 minutes

Cracking egg crumpets (p15)

Chocolate porridge (p21)

Salmon and miso soup (p32)

Greek-style green beans with tomato (p53)

Tomato-chorizo no-stir risotto (p89)

Shake and bake (p93)

Oven-baked bolognese (p99)

Ham, cheese and pickle pasties (p116)

Sausage rolls with onion marmalade (p119)

Sizzling chorizo and prawns (p123)

Stringy tomato pesto omelette (p129)

Perfect for playdates

Three ways with a jacket potato (p28)

Potato parcels (p29)

Salmon and ketchup fishcakes (p31)

Gnocchi bake (p40)

Broccoli pasta (p43)

Friday night pizza (p43)

Meatballs and spinach (p54)

Bish bash bosh burgers (p135)

Ten-second banoffee pie (p137)

Banana ice cream (p147)

Shake your own ice cream (p147))

Five-minute cake-in-a-cup (p148)

Mid-week suppers for grown-ups

Salmon and miso soup (p32)

Gnocchi bake (p40)

Spaghetti alla puttanesca (p42)

Broccoli pasta (p43)

Greek-style green beans with tomato (p53)

Giant couscous and apple salad (p71))

Aubergine, red pepper and fennel seed stew (p72)

Leek and potato pie (p76)

Uncle Brend's apple slaw (p83)

Tomato-chorizo no-stir risotto (p89)

Shake and bake (p93)

Chicken, chorizo and lentils (p96)

The store cupboard is empty

Spaghetti alla puttanesca (p42)

Broccoli pasta (p43)

Gnocchi bake (p40))

Everyday Italian tomato sauce (p39)

Tantrum-averting salmon and dill pasta (p48)

Chickpea soup (p67)

Slack mummy soup (p68)

Tortilla tower (p78)

Tomato-chorizo no-stir risotto (p89)

Banana ice cream (p147)

Shake your own ice cream (p147)

Good enough for your friends

Traditional fish pie with a time-saving twist (p26)

Greek shepherd's pie (p34)

Best ever lamb shanks (p35)

Fabulously fast lasagne (p50)

Pulled pork with apple butter (p58)

Hipster chilli (p60))

Salmon with artichokes and anchovies (p94)

Very simple beef stew (p95)

Mr Plowman's fish stew (p100)

Roast rib of beef (p103)

Rosemary and anchovy leg of lamb (p106)

Aubergine Parmesan with a hazelnut crust (p109)

Emergency roast chicken (p110)

Sizzling chorizo and prawns (p123)

Roasted almonds with rosemary (p134)

Picnics

Spanakopita (p74)

Cherry tomato tart with mozzarella and basil (p98)

Ham, cheese and pickle pasties (p116)

Sausage rolls with onion marmalade (p119))

Potato salad plus (p121)

You might not think your kids will like this, but they will ...

Spaghetti alla puttanesca (p42)

Broccoli pasta (p43)

Slack mummy soup (p68)

breakfast & brunch

By a million miles, breakfast is our favourite meal of the day – partly because after 10 hours with no food, we are just plain hungry, but also because we love its anything-goes attitude. Sweet or savoury, hot or cold, bananas or bacon, the rules are – there are none. Hurrah!

The other good thing about breakfast is that eating loads is encouraged – breakfast like a king, lunch like a prince and dine like a pauper. So pass the chocolate porridge (see page 21)!

With that in mind, meet our Breakfast Pie (see page 18). Basically a fry-up encased in pastry, it's the very essence of brunch – an idea first hit upon by the British in the 1800s as an antidote to a heavy Saturday night. It's the perfect way to kick off a family Sunday – serve it mid-morning and then hit the museums/park/shops. No expensive lunch out required.

Breakfast is one of the few meals where it is easy for families to eat together – it is a good way to set you all up for the day both nutritionally and spiritually. So go on. Tuck into those pancakes and have a family hug. You deserve it!

RASPBERRY, PEAR
and almond muffins

INGREDIENTS

100g (7 tbsp) butter, melted
125ml (½ cup) milk
1 large egg
195g (1½ cups) plain/all-purpose
   flour
30g (⅓ cup) ground almonds
2 tsp baking powder
½ tsp bicarbonate of soda/baking
   soda
pinch of salt
70g (⅓ cup) caster/superfine sugar
110g (scant cup) raspberries
1 pear, cored and chopped
a few flaked/slivered almonds for the
   top of each muffin

Start to finish: 10 minutes prep
+ 20 minutes in the oven

Makes: 12 medium-sized muffins

If we're honest, it's rare that we manage to bake these in time for breakfast – we're much too fond of our sleep. But they are perfect for a fruity brunch. Alternatively, they freeze beautifully, so make them ahead and stick them in the freezer. When you need a tasty breakfast-on-the-go, take one out the night before and it will have thawed by morning.

Preheat the oven to 190°C/375°F/gas mark 5. Place paper muffin or cake cases in a 12-hole muffin tin.

In a small bowl, melt the butter – 30 seconds in the microwave should do it.

Measure the milk out in a jug and add the egg. Whisk with a fork.

In a large mixing bowl, put the flour, ground almonds, baking powder, bicarbonate of soda, salt and sugar. Give it a stir so it's well mixed. Add the fruit and gently stir in. Make a well in the centre. Pour the milk, egg and melted butter into the dry ingredients.

Stir, not too hard, until the batter is just mixed and there aren't any pockets of flour. Unlike a sponge cake, a muffin batter needs to be stirred as little as possible to prevent the texture from being tough. Spoon into the paper cases, filling them two-thirds full. Scatter with flaked/slivered almonds.

Bake for about 20 minutes, depending on your oven. They should be golden brown and a skewer inserted into the centre will come out clean.

Remove from the oven and let them cool for a few minutes before putting them on a wire rack to cool thoroughly.

Let your imagination run wild! The great thing about muffins is that you can put whatever you like in them. Got some apples that need eating? Chop them up and pop them in. Maybe with a dash of ground cinnamon? Plums and ginger? Oh yum! Try blueberries rather than raspberries.

The rule of thumb with this recipe is to use about 200g (about 1½–2 cups) of fruit – dried, fresh, whatever you have, in a combination of your choosing. If any of that fruit is very juicy, reduce the milk slightly. If it's dried, you might need to add a touch more milk.

Lucy

SUPERHERO
breakfast bars

These breakfast bars are very simple and because of the oats and nuts, they release energy slowly, which could help your children concentrate for longer at school. By giving them these for breakfast, they will win a Nobel Prize before they are 11. Probably. Claire calls them posh rice crispy cakes, but I prefer Superhero Breakfast Bars. They may not wear a cape, but are perfect to eat while crime fighting on the school run.

Preheat the oven to 180°C/350°F/gas mark 4. Grease a 20-cm (8-inch) square baking dish and line with baking paper.

Turn the oats onto a baking sheet and pop in the oven for 10 minutes or so until lightly toasted. Toss them with the crisped rice, seeds, nuts and dried fruit in a large bowl.

In a small saucepan, heat the nut butter and honey over a low heat until they just melt. (DO NOT LET THE MIXTURE BOIL! If it does, it will be like glue.) Stir in the cinnamon, then pour it over the oat mixture and stir gently.

Turn into the prepared baking dish and press the mixture evenly and firmly.

Cover and refrigerate until set. Cut into 16 squares or thereabouts.

INGREDIENTS

135g (1 cup) porridge/rolled oats
100g (4 cups) crisped rice cereal or corn flakes (chocolate crisped rice or corn flakes are also fine)
200g (1½ cups) unsalted sunflower seeds (or pumpkin or sesame seeds – whatever you have)
100g (¾ cup) shelled pistachio nuts
150g (1 heaping cup) raisins, sultanas/golden raisins or currants
150g (1 cup) dried sour cherries, cranberries or other dried fruit
250g (1 cup) almond or peanut butter
300g (1 cup) runny honey
2 tsp ground cinnamon

Start to finish: 10 minutes prep + a couple of hours to set in the fridge

Makes: 16 squares

CRACKING EGG *crumpets*

250g (1 cup) cottage cheese
zest of ½ unwaxed lemon
a sprinkling of thyme leaves
a glug of olive oil
1 egg
4 crumpets
knob of butter
100g (3⅓ oz) smoked salmon
black pepper

Start to finish: 10 minutes

Serves: 2 grown-ups,
or 1 grown-up and 2 kids

Hot toasted crumpets have always had a place in my heart (along with the kids and Mr McDonald), but then, along came this. It was different. Special. This was 'eggy crumpets'. Things have changed. Try them and have your world rocked.

First, mix the cottage cheese with the lemon zest, thyme and olive oil. This livens things up no end.

Then crack the egg into a shallow dish, something that the crumpets can lie flat in. Give the egg a brief whisk with a fork to break the yolk up a bit, and place the crumpets in it. Turn the crumpets over, so each side is coated with egg, then remove from the dish as you don't want them to absorb all the egg.

Place a frying pan over a medium heat and add a large knob of butter. Once it's melted and has covered the base of the pan, throw the egg-soaked crumpets in. After a minute on one side, the egg should be cooked and the crumpet browned; turn over and cook the other side. After another minute the crumpet should be heated all the way through, and the egg cooked. Remove from the pan and put on plates.

Spoon the cottage cheese mixture over the crumpets, and place the smoked salmon on top. Serve with a squeeze of lemon and a sprinkle of pepper on top and bingo!

Serve with... The smoked salmon and cottage cheese topping is an attempt at being healthy. Another favourite is bacon and maple syrup for something a bit more decadent.

Claire

BLUEBERRY *crumble cake*

320g (2½ cups) plain/all-purpose flour
200g (1 cup) sugar
170g (1½ sticks) cold unsalted butter
1 tsp bicarbonate of soda/baking
    soda
1 egg
125g (½ cup) plain yogurt
375g (3 cups) blueberries

Lemon glaze (optional)
200g (1¾ cups) icing/confectioners'
    sugar
2–3 tbsp lemon juice

Start to finish: 15 minutes prep
+ up to 1 hour in the oven

Makes: 12 slices

A friend first made this for us for breakfast and it was a revelation. 'Cake for breakfast?', we asked. 'Why not?' she replied. And it's a good question. She makes it for birthday breakfasts in her house and it's definitely a reason to embrace the passing years. It's adapted from an old American cookbook, *The Artist in the Kitchen*, which is full of tasty little gems.

Preheat the oven to 190°C/375°F/gas mark 5. Line and butter a 25-cm (10-inch) round cake tin.

In a large bowl mix the flour with the sugar. Then using your fingertips, rub in the cold butter (see tip below). After a while it should start to look like breadcrumbs, and that's when it's time to stop. Don't worry if it's not completely uniform, it's nice to have a slightly irregular crumble, and better that than to continue rubbing and make the mix gloopy.

Scoop out about 1½ cups of this crumble mixture and put it in a bowl in the fridge. This will be used for the crumble topping, and you won't need it until the end. Stir the bicarbonate of soda/baking soda thoroughly into the remaining mix.

In a separate bowl lightly beat the egg and stir in the yogurt. Stir them into the sugar and flour mixture, and then fold in just under half of the blueberries.

Spread the batter in the prepared dish and scatter the remaining blueberries on top. Take the crumble topping from the fridge and sprinkle it over the top. Bake in the centre of the oven for 50 minutes, or until a skewer comes out of the centre clean.

To make the glaze, mix the icing/confectioner's sugar with just enough lemon juice to make a drizzling consistency.

Serve warm or at room temperature drizzled with the lemon glaze or just dusted with icing sugar.

The colder the fingers, the better the crumble

When making a crumble, think pastry rather than cake. This means the butter (and your hands) should be as cold as possible, rather than room temperature. A good trick for keeping butter cold when rubbing it in is to chop it into smaller bits before you start. This way your fingers don't have to work too hard breaking down a big lump of butter, which would bring up its temperature, and make the crumble more sticky and less, well, crumbly.

BREAKFAST *pie*

INGREDIENTS

2 x sheets all-butter shortcrust pastry (215g/7½ oz each sheet)
1 large onion, chopped
1 x 400g (14 oz) tin of baked beans
a splash of Worcestershire sauce
6 good-quality sausages
6 rashers/slices of streaky bacon
200g (7 oz) black pudding/blood sausage
200g (2¼ cups) grated Cheddar cheese
1 egg
20cm (8 inch) loose-bottomed cake tin

Start to finish: 20 minutes prep
+ 50 minutes in the oven

Serves: 6

This is the ultimate cooked breakfast... baked in a pie. A proper fry-up, although delicious, is the roast dinner of the breakfast world – it is all about timing. First thing in the morning that can be a bit much, so this takes the pressure off. Housed in shortcrust pastry (shop-bought obviously!) are the usual suspects of bacon, sausages and even baked beans. It can be made in advance, meaning you can enjoy the Sunday papers and a Bloody Mary while it cooks. Children love this.

Take the pastry out of the fridge 10 minutes before you need it, otherwise it is difficult to work with and will crack when unrolled.

In a large saucepan, gently fry the chopped onions until they are browned. Drain the beans and give them a quick rinse. You want some of the sauce to stick to them, but not too much, otherwise your pie may end up with a 'soggy bottom'. Add to the onions with a splash of Worcestershire sauce and heat through.

In a separate pan, fry the bacon and sausages (don't use oil, as they should be fatty enough) until they are browned. Chop the bacon into small pieces and slice the sausages. (Don't forget, this can all be done the night before, and it is also a good way of using up leftovers.) Stir the cooked meat into the bean mixture and season – go easy on the salt as the meat will be salty enough. Crumble in the black pudding.

Put the cake tin on one of the pastry sheets and cut around it with a knife. This is your pie lid. Grease the cake tin, line the base with baking paper, and then place the remaining pastry sheet inside. Gently push it down, so it is nice and snug around the bottom and the edges. It won't fit perfectly, but if you trim some of the overhang off you can add it where needed. Smooth out any joins with your fingers. It may look like a patchwork quilt, but don't worry, it will still taste delicious. Pour the filling into the pastry case. Sprinkle on the grated cheese. Place the pie lid on top, and pinch to the sides of the pastry case. Beat the egg and brush the lid with it. Either bake straightaway or put in the fridge.

Preheat the oven to 180°C/350°F/gas mark 4.

Bake for 50 minutes. If you made it the night before, then try to remember to take it out of the fridge an hour before cooking. If you don't, you will need to up the cooking time slightly.

When cooked, remove from the oven and let it stand for 10 minutes, then take the pie in its tin to the table. Balance it on a tin of baked beans (or something similar) and lower the cake tin. People should start to applaud at this point. Transfer to a plate and cut into wedges. It is nice with eggs on the side.

Lucy

The beauty of shop-bought pastry Of course, you can make your own pastry. I am sure it is very therapeutic, but more often than not, I buy mine from the supermarket. Both puff and shortcrust shop-bought pastry are of such high quality that it is almost impossible to tell it's not home-made. If you can, buy the all-butter version, as it tastes even better. It freezes well (just remember to defrost it, although it only takes a couple of hours to thaw in a warm room), and it is a great store cupboard stand-by. If it has been in the fridge, it will need to warm up a bit before you can use it, otherwise, it is prone to cracking. To remove any cracks in the sheet, gently press the pastry together with a finger.

Pastry can be used to make cheese straws, savoury pies, sweet tarts, sausage rolls, pasties, jam tarts – the world's your oyster.

FIG AND APPLE PORRIDGE
for lazybones

INGREDIENTS

150g (1 heaping cup) porridge/rolled oats
250ml (1 cup) apple juice and/or water or – if you don't like measuring – enough sploshes to cover the oats. You can drain off the excess in the morning

Optional toppings
1 apple, grated
a drizzle of honey
chopped dried figs, apricots and a handful of raisins
fresh fruit: blueberries, strawberries, banana
2 spoonfuls of Greek yogurt
toasted hazelnuts or walnuts
a light dusting of ground cinnamon or ginger

Start to finish: 1 minute, once you've soaked the oats

Serves: 2 grown-ups

We're always looking for a shortcut, but when it comes to everyday breakfasts, there seems little chance to deviate from the superfood that is porridge/oatmeal. This involves saucepans first thing in the morning. And stirring. Sigh. However, we have discovered this version of porridge. It is officially called Swiss Bircher Muesli, and takes seconds to put together. Ok, you need to bung some oats and apple juice in a bowl the night before, but it's worth it when you've got a breakfast that is quicker than Weetabix.

The night before, put the oats in a large bowl and pour juice or water over the top. Or do this in the morning, and give the oats half an hour to soak up the juice.

When ready to eat, spoon into individual bowls. That's it. Then it's just a case of garnish. I like to grate an unpeeled apple over it. Much of an apple's nutrients comes from the peel and it gives it a bit of texture. Then add some chopped fruit, a spoonful of yogurt, the nuts, honey, whatever you have in the kitchen.

Serve, with a flourish. Watch jaws drop as your family realise you've veered outside the norm, and served them something which is not quite porridge.

CHOCOLATE *porridge*

1 teacup porridge/rolled oats
   (no-one wants to be messing
   about with scales in the morning)
1 teacup water
1 teacup milk, plus 1 tbsp extra
1 tsp cocoa powder
pinch of salt

Start to finish: 10 minutes

Serves: 2 children

All hail! All hail chocolate porridge! It changes lives. Well, it's changed ours.

Your children may go to bed on time. Ours don't and the promise of this chocolate porridge for breakfast is the perfect bribe to get them to go to sleep. Just make the porridge as you would normally but add cocoa. Easy and life-changing.

Put the oats in a small pan and stick it on the hob/stovetop. Add the water and milk and turn on the heat. Stir regularly to stop the porridge sticking to the bottom of the pan. Keep it on a gentle heat so it doesn't burn or become glue-like.

While it's cooking, mix the cocoa powder and tablespoon of milk in a cup until it makes a chocolatey solution.

After about 5 minutes of cooking, add the salt and the chocolate solution. Cook for a bit longer if you think the oats need it and add more milk if it looks a bit dry. Serve.

Delicious things to eat on your porridge Sometimes we slice up a banana. Chopped pear with crème fraîche is nice or, if we are feeling very kind, a liberal scattering of chocolate sprinkles.

Claire and Lucy

THREE WAYS *with spelt pancakes*

170ml (¾ cup) milk and 1 tbsp
   lemon juice or vinegar (or
   180ml/¾ cup buttermilk)
100g (¾ cup) spelt flour
1 tsp sugar
¼ tsp salt
1 tsp baking powder
¾ tsp bicarbonate of soda/baking
   soda
1 egg, beaten
1 tbsp melted butter, plus extra
   to fry

To serve
a handful of blueberries, Greek
   yogurt and Lemon Curd (see
   page 140), or
about ½ grated apple (skin and all),
   ½ teaspoon ground cinnamon,
   maple syrup, or
sliced bananas, vanilla extract,
   honey

Start to finish: 10 minutes prep
+ 10 minutes cooking

Makes: 10–12

Every day is Pancake Day in our house. My children love making these American-style pancakes and more often than not there is a jug of batter going lightly grey in the back of my fridge (don't be alarmed by the colour; a quick whisk with a fork sorts it out). We have these before school with one of the suggested toppings. Yum!

Combine the milk and lemon juice to make your own buttermilk, unless you have the real stuff. After a couple of minutes it will curdle and sour (see page 186).

In a separate bowl mix together the spelt flour, sugar, salt, baking powder and bicarbonate of soda/baking soda.

Add the egg and melted butter to the curdled milk/buttermilk. It will look revolting but don't be alarmed, the end result will taste delicious! Give it a quick stir and then pour into the flour mixture and give it another quick stir.

Melt some butter in a hot and heavy frying pan. Add spoonfuls of the batter to the pan (the batter should be runny but hold its shape). The pancakes should be about 3cm (1¼ inches) wide – any bigger and they are hard to flip. Cook until the bottom is set and browned and bubbles appear on the top, then flip and cook until browned underneath.

For the blueberry version, just serve the berries on top of the cooked pancakes with Greek yogurt and a drizzle of lemon curd.

For the apple version, mix the cinnamon in with the flour. Grate the apple into the mixture at the end, giving it a quick squeeze first to get rid of excess liquid. Serve with maple syrup.

For the banana version, mix the vanilla extract with the egg. Fold in sliced banana into the mixture at the end. When ladling the pancake batter out, try to make sure you have equal numbers of banana slices per pancake.

The batter will not keep once fruit has been added so use immediately.

Lucy

Flirting with flour I have been experimenting with using different types of flours recently and spelt is a favourite. It has a nutty flavour and is more easily digestible with a higher protein content than ordinary wheat flour, so can often be tolerated by the wheat intolerant. It can be substituted for ordinary flour in most cakes, but you will need to add slightly more liquid as it soaks it up. If you don't want to go the full monty, try half spelt and half plain/all-purpose flour or even just a quarter spelt flour.

BREAKFAST *banana split*

INGREDIENTS

a couple of strawberries (or any
   other berries)
1 banana
150ml (⅔ cup) Greek yogurt
drizzle of honey
flaked/slivered almonds

Start to finish: 5 minutes

Serves: 1

It is amazing how just slicing a banana lengthways, adding some ice cream and a bit of strawberry sauce transforms a piece of fruit into the world's most delicious dessert. We love banana splits so much we even have them for breakfast, replacing the ice cream with Greek yogurt, the strawberry sauce with fresh fruit, and the grated chocolate with flaked/slivered almonds. Obviously children love banana splits. They taste even better when eaten from an authentic banana split dish for breakfast, too – don't ask us why.

Chop up the berries and place on the bottom of your banana split dish. Split the banana lengthways and place it on top. Scoop on the Greek yogurt, drizzle on the honey and sprinkle with some flaked almonds. Smile. Eat.

comfort food

There are days when we all need a little comforting. Important days, back-to-school days, rainy days, or just Tuesdays. They are when, as a parent, all you want to do is wrap your family up and keep them warm with some pillowy mash, cheesy pasta or a comforting soup. These dishes are the culinary equivalent of a roaring fire and slippers.

Traditionally, comfort foods are high in carbs. And although mashed potato is well represented in this chapter, we are proud to say so is fish! And vegetables! We've found some healthy (well, healthier) comfort dishes – we know! What luck.

Our Traditional Fish Pie (see page 26) is everything a fish pie should be – mashed potatoes? Check. Prawns? Check. Peas? Check. It takes a while to make, but it's worth every minute and in a few years your children will be calling you from university, asking for the recipe.

If you want something super fast, and a sure-fire dinner winner for playdates, try our Potato Parcels (see page 29). Potatoes in a foil parcel with bacon – what's not to love? These are the kind of comforting dishes that actually make you hanker for a rainy Tuesday in winter.

INGREDIENTS

olive oil
1 celeriac, peeled and chopped
2 leeks, finely chopped
1 chicken stock/bouillon cube
3 tbsp single/light cream
a dash of truffle oil (optional)
chopped fresh flat-leaf parsley
salt and pepper

Start to finish: 20 minutes prep
+ 20 minutes cooking

Serves: 4

Claire

Celeriacs are the ugly ducklings of the vegetable world. But chop off the strangely stringy bottom, shave off the oddly hairy skin and you have a food of the gods. This soup is delicious, distinctive and delightfully easy to make. It's the perfect winter warmer for a cold day.

I know truffle oil is expensive, and it's not obligatory, but it will transform an already very nice soup into an amazing soup. In fact it transforms pretty much everything it touches – culinary fairy dust.

In a large saucepan splash some olive oil. Put the pan over a medium heat and throw in the celeriac and leeks. Let them cook for 10 minutes, stirring occasionally.

Add enough water to cover the vegetables and crumble in a chicken stock/bouillon cube. Give it a stir and bring it to the boil.

Cover the pan and let it simmer for 20 minutes, until the celeriac is tender.

Using a hand-held blender (so much easier than an upright blender, and you don't have to pour hot liquid from one receptacle to another), purée the soup thoroughly.

When you're ready to serve, stir in the cream. Season with salt and pepper. Serve in soup bowls with a drizzle of truffle oil, if using, and a scattering of parsley.

TRADITIONAL FISH PIE
with a time-saving twist

INGREDIENTS

750g (1¾ lb) red-skinned
  potatoes
400g (about 1 lb) mixed fish
  fillets – a mix of smoked
  and unsmoked haddock
  is traditional. Check the
  frozen food aisle in your
  supermarket (see opposite)
4 peppercorns (optional)
1 bay leaf (optional)
a few splashes of milk
a dash of vegetable oil
bunch of spring onions/
  scallions, finely chopped
150g (5 oz) unshelled
  prawns/shrimp, cooked or
  uncooked, large or small,
  it's up to you
2 tbsp frozen peas
small bunch of flat-leaf
  parsley, finely chopped
200ml (scant 1 cup) full-fat
  crème fraîche
100g (1 packed cup)
  Cheddar cheese, grated
2 hard-boiled eggs
a large splash of milk
chunk of butter
salt and pepper

Start to finish: 40 minutes
prep + 30 minutes in the
oven

Serves: 4

A comforting bowl of mashed potatoes and creamy, cheesy fish – how can that not improve your day? This is a pie to be proud of. Give it to the kids (it's the perfect way to get them to eat fish) or have it for Sunday lunch when friends are over. You can make it in advance and just pop it in the oven when they arrive – no last-minute nervous breakdowns, hurrah! The clever time-saving twist (crème fraîche instead of a roux sauce) means less washing up, too.

Peel and chop the potatoes, then pop them into a large saucepan of salted water. Bring to the boil and cook until tender – usually about 20 minutes.

While the potatoes are cooking, place the fillets in a large frying pan and cover with milk. Add a few peppercorns and a bay leaf, if you have one. Turn the heat on and bring to the boil. Simmer, while keeping a close eye on it, to make sure the milk doesn't boil over. Keep cooking until the fish is opaque.

Once opaque, remove the fish from the milk and flake it off the skin using a fork. While you are doing this, give the fillets a good feel with the tips of your fingers to make sure there are no bones.

Preheat the oven to 200°C/400°F/gas mark 6.

In a frying pan with some vegetable oil, lightly fry the spring onions/scallions until they are translucent.

Add the prawns/shrimp and cook until pink (or let them heat through if they are already cooked). Then throw in the peas. Frying peas – are we crazy? Trust us, it's fine. Pop the fish flakes in and take off the heat.

Add the crème fraîche and about three quarters of the grated cheese, all the parsley, black pepper and a little salt. Chop the boiled eggs roughly and add. Then give the whole lot a stir, trying not to let the fish disintegrate too much, but covering everything with the crème fraîche.

Place the fish in a 2 litre (2 quart) ovenproof dish or 4 individual ramekins.

Take the cooked potatoes off the heat. Mash them until creamy, add milk and butter. Season well with salt and pepper (there's nothing worse than under-seasoned mashed potato, so taste and check).

Place the mashed potato on top of the fish mix and spread over evenly. Using a fork, scrape the potato up and down in lines to make attractive little peaks.

Scatter over the remaining cheese and pop in the oven for 30 minutes, until the top is golden brown. Serve with a salad. And ketchup.

Fabulous frozen fish If you don't have a trusty fishmonger nearby, it might be worth checking out the frozen food aisle of your nearest supermarket. Frozen fish is often much cheaper than fresh, and the chances are it is in better condition too. If you are buying 'fresh' fish, check that it hasn't been previously frozen. If it has, you are just paying more for someone else to defrost it for you. Other advantages of frozen fish is that it is often clearly labelled, so you can check for the MSC tick – the Marine Stewardship Council only 'tick' fish that has been caught sustainably.

THREE WAYS
with a jacket potato

Monday lunchtime is baked potato time. You can set your watch by our spuds. We love that kind of routine in family life – it means no brainpower goes into thinking about lunch. It's just there. Immoveable. Reassuring. But this type of routine is only as good as the jacket spud you serve up. And it's easy to get it wrong.

We blame microwaves. Before they came along it was hard to muck up a jacket potato, but then thin, papery skins became the norm. And just as we were giving up hope of ever getting a decent jacket spud, those huge 'baking potatoes' entered the supermarket; their pockmarked skin remaining thin and tasteless despite several hours in the oven. We had almost accepted that the glory days of jacket potatoes would just be in our memory, and something we could tell our grandchildren about. But then a last-ditch attempt bore fruit. We asked our mum what type of potato she used to bake. 'King Edwards,' she said. 'We used King Edwards for everything.' And so we tried them, and the Monday lunchtime ritual began.

We've since realised that red-skinned potatoes are great too – Maris Pipers and Desiree. (American cooks will find Yukon Gold and Russet potatoes ideal for baking.)

So, what are the tricks?

First catch your potato. We think it's quite nice for the kids to have a whole small potato, and so our potato cooks at the same rate, we have two or three small ones each, rather than one big one. That means more skin – yay! We (olive) oil them, sprinkle with sea salt and pepper, prod a bit with a fork and pop into an oven preheated to 190°C/375°F/gas mark 5. They will be done in an hour, but leave them for longer to get maximum crunch. They shouldn't burn if you leave them in for another half hour or so. In fact, so versatile are these wondrous things, and so perfect for the time-poor parent, oven-baked jacket potatoes actually improve if you leave them on a really low heat for a few hours and go off to a playgroup or coffee morning. This makes the skin even crispier.

Yes, you can partially microwave them, and then bake for a proper skin. But it's more complicated, and you have to work out how long the potato has to go in each according to its size. We'd rather spend that brainpower on working out what to put on our potatoes.

One way

Thinly slice a leek, and fry in a large knob of butter. Once it's translucent, which takes about 5 minutes, stir in a big blob of cream cheese and grind in black pepper. Yum. Even young kids like this.

Two ways

Grated Cheddar (of course) with finely chopped spring onion/scallion and a generous scattering of crispy bacon.

Three ways

This is the most complicated, but it's a good way of incorporating more green stuff if you have to resort to subterfuge. Cook some broccoli florets until soft. When the potatoes are cooked, cut them in half and remove as much of the potato flesh as you can from the skins. Using a fork, add the broccoli to the potato, mashing it until it is green. Stir in some grated Cheddar, butter, salt and pepper. Re-stuff the potato. It is now green. Ta da! Alien potatoes.

POTATO *parcels*

a portion of similarly sized new
  potatoes – you choose how many
  will fill you or your child
olive oil
salt and pepper
1 rasher/slice of bacon, chopped
  very small
butter

Embellishments
To be used in any combination that
  pleases you, but just raid the fridge
  for more ideas:
a couple of chopped spring onions/
  scallions
a handful of frozen peas
a scattering of mint
¼ red onion, sliced
a couple of chunks of goat's cheese
a sprinkling of flat-leaf parsley
a couple of chunks of brie
1 tsp mustard
some halved button mushrooms

Start to finish: 5 minutes prep
+ 50 minutes in the oven

Serves: 1

We may have discovered the perfect playdate meal, the most
inspired throw-it-together supper and the easiest pop-it-in-and-
forget-about-it lunch. And, guess what? There's no washing up.
Not even a plate. Ok, maybe a knife and fork if you don't want
to use your hands.

Preheat the oven to 220°C/425°F/gas mark 7.

Rip a large square of aluminium foil. Smear some butter on it,
in the middle. Rub the potatoes with oil and salt. Place them in
the centre of the foil. If you are in a rush, cut them so they cook
more quickly; just make sure they are all the same size so they
cook at the same rate.

Sprinkle the bacon over the top. Add embellishments. Grind some
pepper over.

Fold the foil up so it forms a parcel. Place on a baking sheet and
pop in the oven for 50 minutes. It may need longer if the potatoes
are big. Remove and check that the potatoes are browned and
cooked through.

Serve the foil parcel opened on a plate (kids love this, eating
straight from the parcel) or transfer to a plate and serve with
your best silver (better for adults). Enjoy and think of all the
time – and washing-up liquid – you have saved!

CREAMY SMOKED HADDOCK *on sourdough toast*

4 smoked haddock fillets
enough milk and water to cover
    the fish in a shallow pan
knob of butter
2 leeks, finely chopped
300ml (1¼ cups) crème fraîche
4 slices toasted sourdough
    bread, buttered
4 soft-boiled eggs
salt and pepper
chopped flat-leaf parsley, to
    garnish

Start to finish: 20 minutes

Serves: 4

Creating this plate of creamy fish on crunchy sourdough is a relaxing meander in the kitchen. It's perfect as an after-school meal for them, or a mid-week dinner for you. Pop the creamy fish on a big pile of fresh watercress for something zingy and healthy. That's a serving suggestion for you, not the kids, obviously. We're not crazy.

Put the haddock fillets in a large frying pan, so they are not overlapping and cover with a mix of milk and water. Place over a medium heat on the hob/stovetop, and cook until the fish is white and opaque.

Flake the fish off the skin, using a fork. This is a good time to double-check for bones. A stray bone can put a kid off fish for life.

In a saucepan – or the same pan if you give it a bit of a rinse – melt the butter. Throw in the leeks and cook until translucent, which should take less than 5 minutes.

Add the flaked haddock fillets and crème fraîche to the pan. Stir until all the ingredients are combined and heated through. Season with salt and pepper.

Serve on top of the buttered toast, with the soft-boiled egg cut in half, and a sprinkling of chopped parsley to garnish.

How to soft-boil an egg We do love a poached egg, but what a faff! With a dash of vinegar here, and 'swirl the water' there. Instead, try soft-boiled eggs. You can make them in advance, which means they are an easy, protein-filled garnish without any of the last-minute stress of their poached compadres. Delia Smith suggests lowering a room temperature egg into a pan of boiling water and letting it simmer for a minute. Then take it off the heat, cover and let it sit for 6 minutes. Even easier than that is to use a colour-changing egg timer. Pop it in the water with your eggs, and its colour lets you know how cooked your eggs are.

Claire

SALMON
and ketchup fishcakes

Have you ever watched a playdate go wrong? It's a horrible, horrible thing. No one is speaking. It all feels a bit Lord of the Flies. You know it's probably because they're all hungry, but food is still half an hour of frantic chopping away. Nope? Just me, then. Well, not anymore! This recipe needs a bit of cooking and mashing earlier on in the day, but when it comes to tea-time, they're ready in less than 10 minutes. That's quicker than fish fingers.

Peel the potatoes and chop into equal sizes. Pop them into a pan with salted water and bring to the boil. Cook them for about 20 minutes, until soft.

After 5 minutes, place a colander with the salmon fillets in it over the pan. Cover the colander with foil or a pan lid and let the fillets steam for about 10 minutes until they are cooked. Meanwhile, zest the lemon and chop the parsley and put into a large bowl.

Once the potatoes are cooked, drain and mash them in the pan with the butter. Put them in the large bowl, add the tomato ketchup and stir in with the zest and parsley. Season with salt, pepper and as much of the cayenne pepper as you dare. The cayenne adds a bit of dimension to the flavour, but you don't want to scare the children.

Flake the salmon, checking for bones. Stir into the mash, without bashing it about too much. Stir the egg in.

Pour some flour onto a plate. Shape the mixture into patties using the palms of your hands. If the mixture is a bit too wet from the egg, stir in a bit of flour. Keep the patties no thicker than 2cm (¾ inch) so they cook through easily. Toss them in the flour on the plate, place on another plate and once you've shaped them all, put it in the fridge. Leave them for at least 30 minutes or more to help them firm up.

When you are ready to cook, heat some oil in a large frying pan. I put in enough so that it's about 2–3mm (about ⅛ inch) deep. When it's hot, put the fishcakes in, probably only about four at a time. Fry on each side until golden, which takes about 3–4 minutes.

The great thing about fishcakes is that the protein and the carbs are all there, so you just need some vegetables. Serve with peas or broccoli. And more ketchup.

500g (18 oz) potatoes (good mashers are best; a red-skinned potato like Maris Piper or Russet)
300g (11 oz) fresh salmon fillets
zest of 1 unwaxed lemon
as much finely chopped flat-leaf parsley as you think you can get away with
knob of butter
2 tbsp tomato ketchup
½ tsp cayenne pepper
1 egg, beaten
plain/all-purpose flour
vegetable oil, to shallow-fry
salt and pepper

Start to finish: 30 minutes low-key prep + 10 minutes frying

Serves: 4

SALMON *and miso soup*

small bunch of spring onions/scallions
2 salmon fillets
100g (3½ oz) dried noodles
handful of edamame beans
miso paste or powder
400ml (1¾ cups) hot water

Start to finish: 10 minutes

Serves: 2

Claire

Is life a bit hectic at the moment? Work crazy? The kids' homework neglected? Don't worry. This dish will make everything better. The salmon is brimming with omega-3s, the fatty acids which make your children cleverer (tick), using miso soup gives you a sense of Zen and inner calm (tick) and the whole thing is knocked up in a few minutes (tick, tick, TICK!). This is great for an 'I'm-a-good-parent, really' meal for them, or a healthy evening dinner for you.

Boil a kettle full of water. Finely chop the spring onions/scallions.

Put a non-stick frying or griddle pan on the heat. Once hot, put the salmon fillets on it, skin-side down; you don't need any oil. Let them cook without prodding or poking, you'll see the dark pink flesh of the salmon get lighter. Once the flesh near the middle has cooked, using a fish slice, turn the fillet over. Let it cook for a little bit longer, 2–3 minutes, ideally keeping the inside of the fillet a little bit darker than the outside.

Use the boiling water in the kettle to fill a saucepan and cook the noodles according to the packet instructions. Throw the edamame beans in at the end to cook for a couple of minutes.

Stir miso powder or paste into 400ml (1¾ cups) hot water. The amount of miso you use is up to you, have a taste and see how strong you want it – check the information on the packet for guidance.

Put the chopped spring onions into the miso to warm them through.

Strain the noodles and edamame beans, and divide them between two bowls. Place the salmon on top of the noodles and pour the miso broth over the top.

GREEK *shepherd's pie*

900g (2 lb) red-skinned potatoes
50g (½ stick) butter
50ml (3 tbsp) milk
1 tbsp Greek yogurt (optional)
a splosh of olive oil
2 large onions, chopped
3 garlic cloves, chopped
600g (1¼ lb) minced/ground lamb
pinch of dried oregano
salt and pepper
100ml (scant ½ cup) lamb or beef
    stock/bouillon
red wine (optional)
200g (7 oz) feta cheese
150g (5 oz) pitted green olives
small bunch of mint, chopped
50g (scant ½ cup) frozen peas

Start to finish: 35 minutes
+ 20 minutes in the oven

Serves: 4–6

Claire

If you asked a Greek shepherd to make a pie, this is surely what he (or she) would come up with. Lamb, mint, olives and feta, it's like a normal shepherd's pie, but better. It's particularly popular with kids, who tend to wolf down adult-sized portions.

Chop the potatoes and put them in a large saucepan of salted water on the hob/stovetop to boil. Peel them first if you prefer your mash to be smooth; however, if you don't mind the rustic version, leave the peel on and remove some of it once the potatoes have boiled. Usually the skin on red-skinned potatoes comes away quite easily after cooking and you can remove some of it by hand.

After 20 minutes or so your potatoes should be cooked. Drain and mash with butter, milk and Greek yogurt for extra creaminess.

Preheat the oven to 200°C/400°F/gas mark 6.

Heat the olive oil in a saucepan over a low heat and fry the chopped onions until soft and translucent, then add the garlic and fry for a further two minutes.

Add the lamb and fry until brown, stirring all the time for 5–7 minutes. Add a few pinches of oregano near the end and stir some more. Season with salt and pepper.

Mix in the lamb or beef stock/bouillon (you could use some red wine here too, if you have any open). Cook for another 5 minutes and then take off the heat. Crumble in the feta and add the olives, mint and frozen peas. Stir.

Tip from the pan into a medium-sized ovenproof dish. Spread the mash over the top and rake with a fork as this makes it crispier and therefore tastier. Pop in the oven. Bake for 20 minutes and serve with a simple salad of cucumber, tomatoes and olive oil.

What a dish! Shepherd's pies, like fruit crumbles, really vary according to the dish you make them in. A large but shallow ovenproof dish gives you more surface area, so that means everyone gets more of the crunchy stuff, whether that's crumble or mash. A deeper but narrower dish will mean there's more depth but less crunch. It will also take marginally longer to cook. So have a think next time you choose your dish, because quite a lot depends on it.

BEST EVER *lamb shanks*

4 lamb shanks
1 bag soffrito (or 2 chopped onions, 3 diced carrots, 3 chopped celery sticks)
4 red or yellow peppers, chopped
2 x 400g (14 oz) tins of chopped tomatoes
300ml (1¼ cups) chicken or beef stock/bouillon
2 bay leaves
few sprigs of rosemary
salt and pepper
1 x 400g (14 oz) tin of chickpeas or cannellini beans

Start to finish: 15 minutes prep + 2–3 hours cooking

Serves: 4 with leftovers

Nothing is more comforting than lamb shanks that are slow-cooked and melt in your mouth. They are simple to cook; just a bit of assembling, before braising on a low heat for a few hours. They are grown up enough for dinner, yet homely enough for a mid-week supper.

Brown the lamb shanks in a very large frying pan (if yours isn't large enough, then fry them in batches). Put to one side.

In a large saucepan (which has a lid), fry the soffrito in some olive oil until it has softened. Add the peppers and fry for a couple more minutes. Add the tomatoes and stock and bring it up to a low simmer. Add the herbs. Season with salt and pepper.

Arrange the lamb shanks in the pan, so they are standing up. The liquid may not quite cover them, but when the lid is on, the steam will keep the protruding bits moist. Pop on a lid and cook on a low heat for 2–3 hours.

About 20 minutes before serving, add either a tin of chickpeas or cannellini beans and cook until they are heated through. Alternatively, serve with jacket potatoes or mash.

leftovers There is a lot of meat on a shank (although they have gone up in price recently, this still makes them good value) so if you are serving this for a family of four, two children could share one. Freeze leftover meat with the sauce for a rainy day. It is delicious shredded over pasta, on top of a jacket potato or in a wrap.

lucy

4 tbsp vegetable oil
1 large onion, finely chopped
1 red chilli pepper, deseeded and finely diced
1 garlic clove, finely chopped
1cm (½ inch) piece fresh ginger, finely chopped
1 tbsp mild curry powder
1 tsp salt
lots of black pepper
1 x 400g (14 oz) tin of chopped tomatoes
1 tbsp tomato ketchup
1 tsp peanut butter
1 x 400g (14 oz) tin of mango slices, syrup drained and reserved
800g (1¾ lb) cooked or raw chicken, chopped into bite-sized chunks
250ml (1 cup) coconut milk
handful of coriander/cilantro, chopped
yogurt, to serve

Start to finish: 40 minutes

Serves: 4–6

UNCLE TRISTAN'S
mild mango chicken curry

This is Uncle Tristan's recipe. Currently childfree (and relishing it), he has time on his hands, so you may notice it's marginally more tricky than some other recipes. But, oh the taste! Fragrant, sweet, delicious; it could be the recipe that converts your child to the curry side. This is great with either fresh or leftover chicken.

Heat 3 tbsp of the oil in a large, heavy-based saucepan over a low heat and sweat the onions until translucent.

Add the remaining oil along with the chilli, garlic and ginger; cook for 2 minutes, stirring. Add the curry powder, salt and pepper; cook for 1 minute and keep stirring.

Increase the heat to medium, add the chopped tomatoes and cook for around 10 minutes, until the sauce has reduced and thickened.

Stir in the tomato ketchup, peanut butter and 1 tsp of the mango syrup; keep cooking until the sauce turns into a thick paste. Then, if you are using raw chicken, add it now and stir into the sauce. Cook for 5 minutes to coat the chicken and seal in the juices. If you are using chicken leftovers, put the chicken into the mixture and go straight to the next stage.

Add the coconut milk, turn up the heat until the sauce starts to bubble, then reduce the heat and simmer for 8 minutes until the curry is a creamy consistency. If the sauce is becoming too thick, add a little more mango syrup. Alternatively, add water if you feel the curry is becoming too sweet.

Chop and stir in the mango slices and simmer for another 2 minutes. Stir in half the chopped coriander/cilantro and season with salt and black pepper to taste.

Serve with the remaining coriander and a dollop of yogurt if you wish, accompanied by a wedge of lime and basmati rice or flatbread.

Converting your children to the curry side To make this palatable to younger kids, or kids who aren't keen on spicy food, leave out the red chilli and make sure you are using mild curry powder. And add more of the sweet mango syrup from the tin if you want to really win the kids over!

pasta, pizza & pesto

Pasta is surely proof there is a God? A foodstuff that just needs to be plonked in boiling water and then decorated with some odds and ends from the fridge is a reason to rejoice!

And then there's pizza, universally adored by grown-ups and children. Making the dough takes an element of organisation, but make double, freeze half and then an extravagant pizza is never far away. Don't have any mozzarella? Turn it into a quattro formaggi by using those nubbins of cheese you have left in the fridge, and maybe throw a few of those capers on too? Necessity is the mother of invention.

Pesto – one minute a yellowing bunch of herbs at the bottom of the fridge; the next, after a whizz of the blender and the addition of nuts, garlic and cheese, it's food gold. It's easy to believe that making your own pesto is a step too far, when the bought stuff is so good. We'd agree, and (as we hope you know by now) we don't believe in making more culinary effort than we have to. But look at homemade pesto as an effective way of using up bits and pieces in the fridge, rather than something you go out of your way to make. An unused bunch of herbs in the vegetable drawer no longer needs to make you feel guilty. Hurrah!

Claire

EVERYDAY
italian tomato sauce

What do we parents owe the Italians? Personally speaking, my sanity, my kids' health and pretty much the contents of my cupboards and fridge. This recipe is based on the classic by Marcella Hazan, the doyenne of Italian food in America. Brilliant in its simplicity, it is perfectly designed for the family cook. It uses just three ingredients, one of which is tinned tomatoes. I know – it's like she's looked inside your kitchen cupboards and worked out a recipe just for you.

Place the tinned tomatoes in a medium-sized saucepan. Add the butter and the onion. Bring to a simmer and let it bubble away for about 45 minutes. Stir occasionally to break up the tomatoes.

Once cooked, fish out the onion; it's just there to add flavour.

Then blitz with a hand-held blender, or keep it chunky, depending on your preferred texture. Season with salt and pepper.

Congratulate yourself on the Italian authenticity of this dish. Feel a little bit smug.

INGREDIENTS

2 x 400g (14 oz) tins of tomatoes
75g (5 tbsp) unsalted butter
1 medium onion, peeled
    and halved
salt and pepper

Start to finish: 5 minutes prep
+ 45 minutes simmering

Serves: 4 grown-ups as a
pasta sauce

Freeze it! Double the quantities above and freeze the excess in little pouches. Then when there is a meal emergency – at least three times a week in my house – you can whip it out and serve on pasta. I recommend fusilli as it gets deliciously coated in the sauce, with a spot of grated Cheddar or Parmesan cheese on top.

Alternatively, if you're really organised and also have some pizza dough (see page 44) in the freezer, you will always be able to whip up a pizza, whatever the circumstances. Which, I think, in many children's eyes makes you the perfect parent.

GNOCCHI
bake

Lucy

This is the ultimate mid-week supper. It is cheap, filling, quick and delicious. I make it every few weeks using up any vegetables that are wilting/stagnating in my fridge. It reminds me of my student days, and is a great dish to teach older children who are flying the nest. If you've never tried them, gnocchi are little potato dumplings, which can be found in most supermarkets. Gnocchi is a Crumbs favourite as it can be stored for ages and takes 60 seconds to cook. Take that, pasta!

Cook the gnocchi in a pan of boiling water as per the packet instructions. They are ready when they all bob to the top of the pan.

Drain and put back in the saucepan (not over the heat) and stir in the passata, sweetcorn and chard. Season. Pour into a 20 x 30cm (8 x 12 inches) baking dish and sprinkle the mozzarella and breadcrumbs over the top.

Bake at 180°C/350°F/gas mark 4 for 30–40 minutes, or until brown on top.

INGREDIENTS

700g (25 oz) gnocchi
680g (2¾ cups) passata/tomato sauce, or see recipe on page 39
handful of sweetcorn/corn kernels
handful of Swiss chard
200g (2 cups) shredded mozzarella cheese (or any other)
handful of breadcrumbs

Start to finish: 5 minutes prep + 40 minutes in the oven

Serves: 4 greedy people with some leftovers

Store-cupboard saviour! Spinach, peas, fried mushrooms and roast peppers all work well here, too. If you want meat, then add some chopped bacon or torn-up ham to the dish.

Gnocchi is also delicious with pesto stirred through (see page 46) and grated Parmesan cheese on top.

200g (7 oz) spaghetti
a splash of olive oil
2 garlic cloves, sliced
pinch of dried chilli flakes (optional)
2 anchovy fillets
1 x 400g (14 oz) tin of tomatoes
1 tbsp capers
handful of black pitted olives
2 tbsp chopped flat-leaf parsley
salt

Start to finish: 15 minutes

Serves: 2 grown-ups

SPAGHETTI
alla puttanesca

Another brilliant Italian staple. Their knack of pulling together a few ingredients to create delicious meals, ready in minutes, means us working parents are forever grateful. This is a great mid-week supper using only store-cupboard staples. Salty, gutsy, with a hint of heat — adjust the chilli levels and your kids might eat it too.

Bring a large pan of water to the boil. Season with salt and cook the spaghetti according to the packet instructions.

Put some oil in a frying pan and fry the garlic for a minute or so. Then add the chilli flakes, if using, and anchovies. Break the anchovies up a bit with a wooden spoon and then add the tomatoes, capers and olives. Simmer the sauce until the pasta is ready.

Drain the pasta and stir in the tomato sauce. Serve, sprinkled with chopped parsley.

Adjust to taste Got loads of anchovies, but only a few capers? Put them in. No black olives, only green? Oh well, stick 'em in. If we're not going for Neapolitan authenticity, this dish will take just about anything you (or your cupboard) can throw at it. Its strong flavour means you can adjust the quantities of most of the ingredients to suit your taste or the contents of your cupboard, and you still get a delicious salty, tomatoey plate of loveliness.

Claire

200g (7 oz) pasta – they (the
   Italians) say it should be
   orecchiette, we say whatever you
   have in the cupboard
250g (9 oz) broccoli florets
a few glugs of olive oil
2 garlic cloves, sliced
dried chilli flakes to taste (optional)
pinch of sea salt
a glug of cream would be nice,
   but not essential
pepper
Pecorino or Parmesan cheese,
   to taste

Start to finish: 12 minutes

Serves: 2 (hungry) grown-ups

BROCCOLI *pasta*

Who would have thought such a prosaically named dish could inspire such a long-term love affair? One or other of us has been cooking this dish once a week for the past eight years. Its quantities and ingredients may vary, but the comfort, warmth and glow it inspires are always the same. We know being too free with a true love isn't very sensible, but what can we say? We're generous. Fill your boots.

Bring a large pan of salted water to the boil. Put the pasta in. After about 5 minutes, add the broccoli and let it cook with the pasta for the remaining time. We're sure this is sacrilege if you are Italian or a chef, but it saves time and washing up, which are big priorities with family cooking. When the pasta is ready, the broccoli will also be cooked, probably a bit more than you're used to, but that's good.

Strain everything in a colander and leave while you heat the olive oil in the pasta saucepan. You need a fair amount of olive oil as you want it to coat the pasta – two good glugs should do it.

Then cook the garlic (and optional chilli) for a minute, but don't allow it to go brown. Turn off the heat and add the pasta and broccoli and a pinch of salt. Put the lid on the pan and bang it about a bit. The idea is that the slightly soft broccoli breaks up and coats the pasta. Alternatively, give it a good stir to break it up with a wooden spoon. If you have some cream, stir in a bit, add loads of black pepper and serve, sprinkled with grated cheese.

500g (3½ cups) strong white bread
   flour, plus a little extra
2 tsp fast-action dried yeast
2 tsp salt
olive oil
2 tsp honey or sugar

Start to finish: this requires a
little effort and involves different
stages but don't let that put you
off. It is time-consuming, but once
you've developed a routine it takes
little headspace. Allow about
20 minutes hands-on preparation
plus proving and cooking time

Makes: approx 4 pizzas

FRIDAY NIGHT *pizza*

We always have pizza on a Friday. After a week of work and school it is comforting not to have to think about what to eat, for the pizza dough has been rising since lunchtime. It is a family ritual and one I hope will continue ad infinitum. At the moment we have two sittings. Them at 6, often with friends. Us at 9, often with wine. OK, always with wine. The only decision needed is what to put on top (suggestions overleaf) and what to watch on the telly.

Making the dough Mix the flour, yeast and salt in a big bowl (or a food mixer bowl if you are using one). Spoon the olive oil and honey or sugar into a measuring jug and top up with warm water to just over the 300ml (1¼ cups) mark. Make sure the water is not too hot; otherwise the yeast, added in the next stage, won't work (it's magic). Stir well.

Lucy

Kneading by hand Slowly pour the liquid into the flour a little at a time. Either with a wooden spoon or your hands, work the mixture together until you have a soft dough. If it is too sticky, add more flour; if too dry, more warm water.

Turn the dough out on a floured worktop and – biceps ready – start kneading. Pin down part of the dough with one hand and use the heel of the other hand to stretch the dough away from you on the work surface. Then fold the dough back on itself and give it a quarter of a turn. Then another quarter. Then another quarter. And another. In fact quite a few more quarters. After about 10 minutes (arms aching yet?!) the dough will be more supple and will start to bounce back when you prod it. Hurrah! It's done.

Kneading with a food mixer This is much quicker, although a less sensual, hands-on experience. Pour the liquid into the bowl containing the flour, yeast and salt and using the dough hook attachment, start mixing until everything is combined and you have a plump dough – this will take about 5 minutes.

Let it prove Now the fun bit: cover with a damp tea/dish towel and leave to rise, ideally somewhere warmish but not too hot. To prove, the dough has to double in size. Officially, if you have all day or overnight, you should let it prove in the fridge as this slows down the process. I leave mine all day in a warm kitchen and return from the school pick-up to a big puffy dough-creature. When it is proved, my children take it in turns to punch the dough and flatten it out. Whenever I have a go, I find it satisfying, but oddly never as cathartic as I expect. I obviously need a proper punchbag instead.

Get it into shape Next, you need to knead it briefly again. This time just for about a minute or so, or 30 seconds with a dough hook. Then allow it to rise again – this time for about 30 minutes.

Cut it into four pieces with a knife. Try to make the pieces roughly the same shape as the pan you are baking the pizzas in. This sounds weird, but it is then easier to roll into the right shape. I always bake my pizza in rectangular baking trays, after an Italian friend told me it was much easier.

You may see pizza chefs flinging dough around to sculpt something quite perfect. I don't know how they do that, because I have tried and failed so now always roll mine out on a lightly-floured worktop. I then transfer it to the baking tray, where I continue to roll it out until it reaches the edges. I can usually get four pizzas out of this amount of dough if I make the crust thin enough.

Toppings Smother the pizza base with Everyday Italian Tomato Sauce (see page 39) or tomato purée/paste and your preferred toppings. Unlike a sandwich, less is more with a pizza. If you laden it with fillings, it will have a soggy bottom and be too top heavy.

Our favourite pizza toppings are capers (always capers!), blue cheese, salami, spring onions/scallions, halved lengthways, mini mozzarella balls and pesto.

Baking In a move that will shock pizza chefs everywhere, to make sure the bottom cooks properly, I put each pan on the hob/stovetop for about 20 seconds on a medium heat and blast the pizza base from underneath, before baking at 240°C/475°F/gas mark 8 for 10 minutes. Cook until the cheese is brown and bubbling. If the base is still soft, remove it carefully from the pan and put it directly on the oven rack for a couple of minutes until crisp.

about 30g (1 oz) leaves/herbs
40g (scant ½ cup) grated Parmesan cheese
½ garlic clove, crushed
40g (heaping ¼ cup) nuts, lightly toasted
pinch of salt
grind of pepper
75ml (⅓ cup) extra-virgin olive oil
squeeze of lemon (optional)

Start to finish: 5 minutes

Serves: 4

SUNDAY NIGHT
pesto

Why, oh why would we make our own pesto? Are we crazy, when the shops make such a great version? Hear us out. Homemade pesto is a thing apart. Delicious, and a proper meal in a way that pasta and shop-bought pesto just isn't. But, on top of that, it's the best way to use the wilting basil, rocket/arugula or spinach you over-optimistically bought for the weekend. Just blitz it with some odds and ends in your cupboard, and ta da! A delicious condiment is born.

This is a very rough recipe for any variety of pesto you fancy. As you make it, taste, and then add a little bit more of what you fancy to get the perfect pesto for you.

Place the herbs, grated cheese, crushed garlic and the nuts (cooled, after their toasting) in a food processor. Whizz up, season and add the oil. Taste. Add more of what you fancy, and a squirt of lemon juice.

This will keep for a couple of weeks in a lidded jar in the fridge – just make sure there is a layer of oil over the top. Alternatively, freeze in ice cube containers and pop in a freezer bag for long-term storage.

Serving suggestions Spread on sandwiches, stirred into soup, added to salad dressings, drizzled on meat, draped over vegetables. And pasta.

Variations
• parsley, walnuts and Stilton
• rocket/arugula, pine nuts and Parmesan
• basil, pine nuts and Parmesan
And if you don't have Parmesan? Try Pecorino, or *whisper it* Cheddar. Any hard cheese is going to taste pretty good. And mix your herbs if you don't have enough of one type. Basil and parsley, even spinach and basil will work – just don't tell the kids.

Storing herbs There are few things that bring on stronger feelings of culinary guilt than wilted herbs in the fridge. That's why this recipe is such a goodie – even wilted herbs taste good in pesto, just draw the line at anything yellowing or slimy.

Another way to reduce those feelings of guilt is to store your herbs properly so they last longer, giving you more opportunities to use them. Take 3–4 sheets of newspaper and wrap the herbs in them, folding at the ends so they are completely sealed. This will prolong the herbs for a few more days. It also obscures the herbs, so if they do wilt, at least you don't have to see them do it.

TANTRUM-AVERTING
salmon dill pasta

INGREDIENTS

100g (about 1½ cups) quick-cook
   pasta (any variety you like)
50g (½ cup) smoked salmon
   trimmings
2 tbsp crème fraîche
pepper
squeeze of lemon
small bunch of chopped dill,
   flat-leaf parsley or chives,
   whatever you have in
   the fridge

Start to finish: 5 minutes – honest!

Serves: 2 children or 1 grown-up

Why are they crying? And clutching their tummies? Oh yes! You've forgotten to feed the kids again. Never fear. This dish takes less than five minutes to whip up – the joy of quick-cook pasta – and with a little forethought, you can have all the ingredients in your fridge/freezer/cupboard. So get them to stop gnawing the bannister, lunch is ready!

Put the pasta into a saucepan of boiling salted water on the hob/stovetop over a high heat. Let it simmer for 3 minutes (or the length of time specified on the packet) and then drain, keeping a bit of the cooking water back.

Remove from the heat. Stir in the salmon trimmings, crème fraîche and some black pepper. Add a little of the cooking water to loosen things up a bit, if needed, and squirt a bit of lemon juice in. Serve, scattered with chopped herbs.

Miracle Quick-cook pasta – it really does exist. Done in 3–5 minutes, this pasta doesn't appear to have any additional ingredients compared to normal pasta. Perhaps it has been infused with magic? Sold in most supermarkets, it is marginally more expensive. But what does that matter when it comes to a toddler's tantrum? Cheaper than the psychiatrist's bills.

Speed Another way to cook pasta more quickly is to forget that rule of using a big saucepan of boiling water. Instead fill a frying pan with water. The larger surface area means the water gets hotter more quickly. Pop the pasta in and bring to the boil. You'll have to stir fairly regularly to stop it all sticking together, but it should be ready quicker than the recommended cooking time.

Budget Have you ever come across smoked salmon trimmings? They are the cheaper cousin of traditional smoked salmon and most supermarkets sell them. They freeze beautifully, and are perfect to whip out for a Sunday brunch of scrambled eggs and smoked salmon, or a pasta lunch like this.

Cheat If you have crème fraîche in your fridge, use that. If not, why not try cream cheese (you'll need to use a spot more cooking liquid to loosen it up) or Greek yogurt? All are perfect for this dish. We use all three pretty much interchangeably when cooking.

CHERRY TOMATO
basil and pine nut pasta

INGREDIENTS

500g (18 oz) cherry tomatoes
olive oil
400g (14 oz) pasta (penne is nice)
50g (½ cup) toasted pine nuts
100g (1 cup) freshly grated
    Parmesan cheese
basil leaves
salt and pepper

Start to finish: 5 minutes prep
+ 40 minutes cooking

Serves: 4

This is a long-standing family favourite. Roasting the tomatoes gives them a sweet smokiness that goes beautifully with the basil and pine nuts. The sweet bursts of cherry tomatoes are wonderful, but you could use chopped bigger tomatoes here too.

Preheat the oven to 180°C/350°F/gas mark 4.

First, roast the tomatoes. Cut them in half, toss them with olive oil and salt and pepper in a bowl, so they are evenly coated, and then spread them out in a lined roasting tin. (We have only just started making the effort to line roasting tins and it does make washing up much easier.)

Roast them until they are lightly charred and sweet – about 40 minutes. Around 10 minutes before you want to eat, cook the pasta according to the packet instructions. Drain it, reserving a ladleful of cooking water for the sauce. Transfer back to the saucepan and keep warm.

When the tomatoes are roasted, add them to the pasta with the pine nuts, half the Parmesan and the ladleful of the pasta water. Stir until everything is evenly coated, tear the basil and add it to the pan with some salt and pepper. Serve with the remaining Parmesan cheese.

FABULOUSLY *fast lasagne*

INGREDIENTS

Tomato sauce
1 x 400g (14 oz) tin of chopped
    tomatoes
1 tsp sugar
1 tbsp tomato purée/paste
1 small courgette/zucchini, grated

Pork ragù
a splosh of olive oil
450g (1 lb) minced/ground pork
    or sausage meat
1 carrot, grated
2 tsp fennel seeds
½ tsp dried chilli flakes (optional)
2 garlic cloves, crushed
salt and pepper
200ml (scant 1 cup) crème fraîche

4 sheets of dried lasagne
125g (4 oz) mozzarella cheese

Start to finish: 10 minutes prep
+ 20–30 minutes in the oven

Serves: 4

Who can deny the gorgeousness of lasagne? But, oh, the faff! First, cooking the meat, then making a white sauce, before layering the whole caboodle and sticking it in the oven. It's three meals in one. But then, courtesy of a Mary Berry recipe, we discovered lasagne doesn't need to have a white sauce. In fact, just a cursory browning of pork mince, the mixing of some tomatoes, and ta da! Here is our version – a gorgeous layered pasta dish, which takes minutes to make and is still worthy of the name lasagne! Thanks Mary, for the inspiration.

Preheat the oven to 190°C/375°F/gas mark 5.

First, make the sauce. In a bowl or jug, empty the tin of tomatoes. Add the sugar, tomato purée/paste and grated courgette/zucchini. Stir.

Splosh a tablespoon of olive oil into a medium-sized saucepan. Place on the hob/stovetop and heat. Add the pork and stir. Let it cook for a couple of minutes. Once it has some colour, add the carrot, fennel seeds, chilli flakes, garlic, salt and pepper and crème fraîche. Bring to the boil and let it simmer for a couple of minutes.

In a 2-litre (2-quart) ovenproof dish, put a third of the tomato sauce. Then put half the pork mix over the top. Lay a sheet of lasagne over the top. Shred the mozzarella and layer it over the top of the lasagne.

Place the next third of tomato sauce over the cheese, then the rest of the pork mix, a layer of lasagne, the final third of tomato sauce and a thin layer of mozzarella.

Place in the oven for 20–30 minutes. Remove when the top is bubbling and golden.

Seasoning sausages For this dish you could buy either minced/ground pork or sausage meat, or good-quality sausages that you pop out of their skins. If you are buying sausages or sausage meat, it will already be seasoned, so remember you will need less salt and pepper. If you are using pork mince, season it well.

MACARONI CHEESE
with parmesan leek crumbs

INGREDIENTS

400g (14 oz) dried macaroni
75g (5 tbsp) butter, plus extra
    for greasing
50g (heaping ⅓ cup) plain/
    all-purpose flour
900ml (3¾ cups) whole milk
pinch of English mustard powder
100g (1 cup) strong Cheddar
    cheese, grated
1 leek, sliced
2 tbsp grated Parmesan cheese
large handful of breadcrumbs
salt and pepper

Start to finish: 15 minutes prep
+ 10 minutes cooking time

Serves: 4

Macaroni cheese is the daddy of all comfort foods. Its unchallenging simplicity is sometimes just what the doctor ordered when you are having one of those days/weeks/lives. There have been legions written about the best way to make it, which is the best recipe and who invented it. Although it owes its 21st-century popularity to America, by origin it's a French dish but it was popular in Victorian Britain. This is our version. A simple, cheesy, comforting dish that makes everything seem automatically better. Or your money back. Promise! To be eaten on the sofa with a spoon, in dressing gown and slippers.

Cook the macaroni as per the packet instructions, then drain and rinse it. This will get rid of the starch and will stop it sticking together when grilled/broiled.

Melt 50g (3 tbsp) of the butter in a saucepan, and stir in the flour using a wooden spoon. Cook, stirring, for a couple of minutes, then gradually add the milk using a whisk until you have a smooth sauce. Cook until it thickens, stirring constantly, then add the mustard and stir in the Cheddar until smooth (for more details on making the perfect white sauce, see page 64). Remove from the heat and season with salt and pepper.

Preheat the grill/broiler to high.

Pour the macaroni into the sauce and stir so everything is coated and the macaroni is heated through. Tip into a shallow greased baking dish. Fry the leek in the remaining butter until soft. Remove the pan from the heat, add the Parmesan and breadcrumbs and stir. Sprinkle the leek mixture over the top and grill for about 10 minutes until golden and bubbling.

CHAPTER 4

cooking ahead

If you are anything like us, you'll rise before the rest of the family in time for your daily yoga stretches and a quick browse of the international pages of the *New York Times*. Then, before your gorgeous children awake from their slumber, you'll open your perfectly arranged fridge (no liquefied lettuces here) and take out all the ingredients you need to make that night's supper. There's nothing like getting ahead!

What do you mean your life's not like that? Tssskk! Um, OK, nor is ours. People are often mildly shocked when they discover that we regularly have nights when the cupboard is bare and both inspiration and food are in short supply.

That is why cooking ahead is such a good idea. Making a big batch of something like our lovely Hipster Chilli (see page 61) on a Sunday night (half to be frozen, half for Monday night's dinner) helps you feel in control, like a better parent, like you not only read the manual, but wrote it. This chapter is full of recipes that fit that bill. Smug? You betcha!

100ml (scant ½ cup) olive oil
2 small onions, chopped
1 garlic clove, chopped
1 tsp dried thyme
750g (26 oz) green beans
(I use frozen)
2 x 400g (14 oz) tins of tomatoes
250ml (1 cup) water
2 tsp sugar
salt

Serve with
toast
200g (7 oz) feta cheese,
crumbled

Start to finish: 10 minutes prep
+ 45 minutes cooking

Serves: 4

GREEK-STYLE
green beans with tomato

Until recently, green beans were neglected in our house. But then we discovered green beans, Greek-style. Slowly braised in tomatoes, with garlic and onions, served on crusty toast with a sprinkling of feta cheese. It's a delicious hot lunch, or make it in advance and have cold as a vegetable side dish you can keep in the fridge and serve through the week.

Put the oil in a large pan and heat it on the hob/stovetop. Once hot, throw in the onion and, a few minutes later, the garlic. Cook until they are translucent, then add the thyme, green beans, tomatoes, water, sugar and salt.

Bring to the boil, then let it simmer for about 45 minutes. You want the beans to be really tender. That means they will lose their gorgeous green colour and go a slightly paler tone, but what they lose in colour they more than make up for in flavour.

While the beans are simmering, crumble the feta in a bowl using a fork and make the toast. Half a clove of garlic wiped on one side of the toast is a tasty addition. When the beans are ready, serve on the toast and sprinkle over the feta.

Fresh or frozen? Green beans freeze brilliantly, so buy them from the freezer aisle of the supermarket. This way you won't be disappointed by the expensive, imported, slightly chewy variety that are often available fresh.

Claire

Lucy

MEATBALLS
and spinach

Eating meatballs makes me feel thoroughly Italian and like I have stepped off the set of *The Sopranos*. I am not sure how authentic this recipe is (with my ginger hair and glow-in-the-dark skin there is not a millilitre of Roman blood in me), and I am sure real Italian mamas would baulk at me buying meatballs instead of making them from scratch, but it is inarguably my children's favourite meal.

I make a large pot, serve the children and then reheat the rest later for our dinner, stirring in some frozen spinach for one of my five-a-day. If your kids eat green stuff, then congratulations! You can add it earlier. Mine draw the line firmly at peas.

Fry the onion in some olive oil in a large saucepan. Add the passata/tomato sauce, garlic, sugar, salt and pepper. Bring to the boil, and then simmer for as little as 10 minutes, or as long as you've got. The sauce will soon reduce, so it is thick and yummy.

When you're happy with the sauce, pop in the meatballs and stir gently, making sure each one is covered by the sauce. Heat until the meatballs are brown and cooked all the way through (approximately 3–5 minutes). Stir in the spinach, if using.

Serve with spaghetti or rice and lots of grated Parmesan cheese. You can also use lamb meatballs – if so, try stirring a can of chickpeas through the sauce instead of serving with pasta or rice.

INGREDIENTS

1 onion, chopped
olive oil
380ml (1½ cups) passata/tomato sauce
2 garlic cloves, chopped
2 tsp sugar
600g (1¼ lb) beef meatballs (sold in many supermarkets, sometimes on the deli counter). Of course, you can make your own… but then this wouldn't qualify as fast food!
75g (2½ oz) frozen spinach (or a large handful of fresh)
salt and pepper

Start to finish: 5 minutes prep + 10 minutes (or longer) cooking time

Serves: 4

Freezing You can make the sauce in advance (it freezes well), and then just reheat it, popping in the meatballs at the last minute as they take just a few minutes to cook through in the sauce.

SWEET POTATO
and wild rice soup

olive oil
1 onion, chopped
1 tsp red curry paste
1 litre (1 quart) chicken stock/
   bouillon
700g (1½ lb) sweet potatoes, peeled
   and diced
handful of wild rice
80g (3 oz or ½ small tin) coconut
   cream
chopped coriander/cilantro, to serve

Start to finish: 10 minutes prep
+ 30 minutes to cook

Serves: 6

This is love in a bowl. It is a soup for days when it's cold outside and you need warming up. It is the perfect food to cook on a quiet Sunday night, when you want to get ahead of the coming week. It's also great for freezing.

In a large saucepan lightly fry the onion in the oil and when softened, add the curry paste. Next, add the chicken stock and sweet potatoes. Bring to the boil and then simmer for about 30 minutes until the potatoes are soft.

Whizz until smooth in a blender. You may need to do this in two batches as there is quite a lot.

(If you want to freeze this, do so after blending and then simply add the coconut cream after defrosting and reheating.)

When you are ready to eat it, cook the wild rice as per the packet instructions. You just need a handful, as the rice is going to sit in the bottom of the bowl or cup to add texture and bulk.

Pour the soup back into a saucepan and heat, stirring in the coconut cream. Serve with a spoonful of rice in each bowl and coriander/cilantro sprinkled on top.

Lucy

THE THIGH'S
the limit

8 chicken thighs (we prefer skinless, bone out, but whatever your preference)

And then one of these marinades…

Lemon and garlic
juice of 1 lemon (you can keep the peel in too)
2 garlic cloves, crushed
a glug of olive oil
salt and pepper

Yogurt and herb
150g (⅔ cup) Greek yogurt
1 tsp thyme leaves, chopped
1 garlic clove, crushed
a glug of oil
salt and pepper

Honey and soy
2 tbsp honey
6 tbsp soy sauce
juice of 1 lemon (you can keep the peel in too)
1 garlic clove, crushed
a glug of sesame oil

Start to finish: 5 minutes prep, up to 24 hours marinating + 30–40 minutes in the oven

Serves: 4

Are you a leg or a breast person? Breast, although pretty to look at, doesn't have the succulence or flavour of the thigh in our humble opinion. We often have a freezer bag of thighs marinating in the fridge waiting to be roasted, for a simple, no-thought-necessary mid-week supper. Favourite marinade combinations include lemon and garlic, yogurt and herb, honey and soy, but as ever, we encourage you to experiment. Go on!

Mix the marinade ingredients together. Put the chicken thighs in a freezer bag and pour in the marinade. Through the plastic, work the marinade into the meat with your fingers. Leave for a couple of hours, but ideally overnight in the fridge for a stronger flavour.

Preheat the oven to 180°C/350°F/gas mark 4. Line a roasting tin with aluminium foil or baking paper (otherwise you will be chiselling roast chicken bits off the bottom).

Empty the freezer bag into the tin (you can roast the lemon peels, if your marinade contains them, alongside the thighs for a stronger flavour). Space out the meat evenly and roast for 30–40 minutes until cooked through.

These are also good cold in the next day's packed lunch.

PULLED PORK *with apple butter*

INGREDIENTS

3kg (6½ lb) shoulder of pork, skin scored by your butcher
handful of sea salt
burger buns or bread rolls, to serve

Apple butter
big knob of butter
4 cooking apples, peeled, cored and chopped
2 tsp balsamic vinegar
2 tsp Dijon mustard
4 tsp dark muscovado sugar/ dark brown molasses

Start to finish: for the pork, 5 minutes prep + 9–24 hours in the oven; for the apple butter, 30 minutes start to finish

Serves: 10

Pulled pork must be the perfect Crumbs recipe. There is virtually no preparation; the wondrous transformation from raw meat to food-of-the-gods is entirely due to sticking it in the oven. It's a fantastic meal to lazily eat at the weekend and the leftovers can be frozen for a range of delicious meals during the weeks to come.

Preheat the oven to 125°C/250°F/gas mark ½.

Place the pork in a large roasting tin, skin-side up. Rub the skin with kitchen paper to get it really dry. Take a scoop of salt and rub it over the skin, trying to get it into the scores carved by your butcher.

Cover the joint with foil and pop it in the oven for 9–24 hours (such flexibility!). For more information, check out timings below.

An hour or so before you are ready to eat, put the pork in a clean baking tray without the foil (so the fat in the old baking tray doesn't burn and smoke out your kitchen). Turn the oven temperature right up to 220°C/425°F/gas mark 7 and let it cook for 30 minutes to brown the skin. If it hasn't puffed up enough to make good crackling, give it another 10 minutes, but keep an eye on it, as it can burn quite quickly at this stage. Take it out of the oven and let the joint rest until it is cool enough to 'pull' the meat off. Serve in buns with apple butter.

Apple butter

Melt the butter in a saucepan and then add the cooking apples. Add the vinegar, mustard and sugar and let the apples cook away until they lose their shape and become similar to purée. Give them a squash and a bash with a wooden spoon to help them on their way, and keep giving an occasional stir, for around 20 minutes on a low heat, letting the flavours intensify.

The rub

There are many, many different recipes for complicated rubs to put on your pork shoulder. But in my experience, after several hours in the oven, they all taste the same, so I like to keep it simple and just use salt.

Timings

This is a big bit of meat, and you want to cook it long and slow. After 9 hours it will be cooked and come off the bone easily, but you won't be able to cut it with a spoon. If you have more time, leave it for longer. You should be able to leave it in the oven, cooking at such a low temperature for up to 24 hours! This is the ultimate in flexible cooking.

Leftovers

After a meaty weekend, portion up the rest of the pulled pork and freeze it (see page 65). Then when you are ready for more pork, defrost a portion and heat it gently (cover your ears, pulled pork aficionados!) on the hob/stovetop with a splash of apple juice. Alternatively make pork hash with potatoes, mustard and some cabbage on the side. Or mix it up with beans and make a chilli. Really, the options are endless.

2 tbsp olive oil
100g (3½ oz) chorizo
500g (18 oz) minced/ground beef
2 onions, chopped
2 garlic cloves, finely chopped
1 tsp ground cumin
1 tbsp cocoa powder
1 tsp ground cinnamon
1 tsp cayenne pepper
1 tsp brown sugar
1 x 400g (14 oz) tin of tomatoes
300ml (1¼ cups) beef stock/bouillon
2 x 450g (16 oz) tins of haricot/navy
    beans, rinsed
tortillas, coriander/cilantro, crème
    fraîche and lime wedges, to serve

Start to finish: 20 minutes prep
+ 1 hour cooking

Serves: 4

HIPSTER chilli

Forget the pallid chilli of the '80s served on a bed of rice. This is street-food chilli served in tortillas with coriander/cilantro and lime on the side. It's the kind of stuff eaten at a pop-up cafe where the cocktails are served in jam jars and the waiters have beards. Yes, cooking this will make you cool. Briefly. Which I'm sure your 2-year-old will really appreciate. It is also great for making in advance and serving to friends. It means you really will be cool (rather than hot and bothered) when they turn up.

Heat a little oil over a low heat, and throw in the chorizo. Let it cook a little then add the minced/ground beef. Let it brown, giving it a stir all the while. When it has browned, tip the meat onto a plate, put a bit more oil in the pan and add the chopped onions and garlic. Fry for about 10 minutes, until they are soft and translucent, with a hint of caramelisation.

Put the meat back in the pot, and then add the cumin, cocoa powder, cinnamon, cayenne pepper and brown sugar and stir until they are evenly distributed.

Stir in the tomatoes and add the beef stock/bouillon. Bring to the boil, then leave it on a fast simmer for about 45 minutes, so it reduces. You want the chilli to be sloppy, but not too liquidy.

About 10 minutes before you are ready to serve, throw in the rinsed haricot/navy beans and cook.

Serve with warmed tortillas with coriander/cilantro, crème fraîche and a wedge of lime.

Whoah! This isn't hot by grown-up standards, but if you're serving to kids, use just half a teaspoon of cayenne pepper. Add some more to yours at the end of cooking if you want to pep it up a bit.

Warm those tortillas So easy. Just turn on your biggest hob flame/burner. Throw a tortilla on it and count to three. Using kitchen tongs, pick up the tortilla, turn over and count to three again. Pick up with tongs and fold inside a clean tea/dish towel and heat up the rest of the tortillas.

Claire

Claire

POACHED *chicken*

Roast chicken is one of my favourite meals, but occasionally I manage to practise some restraint and rather than roast a chicken and devour every last morsel in one sitting, I poach. Its appeal is delicate and fragrant. The clear broth and succulent flesh make it a delicious and sensible thing to put together mid-week as you can use the meat and stock in other meals. Poached chicken is not a Sunday afternoon showstopper like its roasted cousin, but a Tuesday night, money-in-the-bank supper, for when you want to get ahead.

Put your largest pot on the hob/stovetop and place the chicken in it. I have done this with skin on and skin off and surprisingly there isn't a huge difference, but if you want it to be low fat, remove the skin. Add the lemon, thyme, parsley, leek, celery, peppercorns and garlic. Pour enough water to cover the chicken and the vegetables – probably about 3 litres (4 quarts). Season really well. Turn up the heat and bring to the boil. Simmer gently for about 50 minutes.

Using a slotted spoon, remove as many of the veg around the chicken as possible. They were there to flavour the broth and by now they will be pretty tasteless and not very pretty so just discard. Season the broth again with salt and pepper.

Throw in the fennel and potatoes, and let them simmer with the chicken for 20 minutes or so, until the potatoes are tender. Remove the chicken (when the leg comes away easily from the body, it is cooked) and add the peas and beans. Cook for 3–4 minutes.

Shred some of the chicken. Fish out the potatoes, fennel, peas and beans using the slotted spoon. Divide them up and serve on four soup plates. Distribute the shredded chicken on top of the vegetables. Ladle a couple of spoonfuls of broth onto each plate – there should be loads left. Add a squirt of lemon juice to each plate, and a liberal scattering of dill. Serve, happy in the knowledge you've got at least three more meals to come from that chicken.

More meals from your chicken The tasty broth can plump up a vegetable risotto or work on its own as a soup – just add ginger, chilli, spring onions/scallions, pak choi/bok choy, lemongrass and noodles for a zingy alternative to 'cold medicine' from the pharmacist.

The chicken meat can be used to flavour many other meals. And cooking a whole chicken and portioning it out is so much cheaper than buying breasts/thighs/drumsticks separately. Add a little to flavour the Leek and Potato Pie on page 76 and use shredded chicken instead of refried beans in the Tortilla Tower on page 78. Or put it in Uncle Tristan's Mild Mango Chicken Curry, page 36.

INGREDIENTS

the largest chicken you can
    fit in your pot
1 lemon, cut in half
3 sprigs of thyme
small bunch of flat-leaf parsley
1 leek, roughly chopped
3 celery sticks, roughly chopped
some peppercorns
3 garlic cloves
salt and pepper

To serve
1 fennel bulb, sliced
600g (1¼ lb) new potatoes
100g (⅔ cup) frozen peas
100g (¾ cup) green beans
    (I use frozen)
juice of 1 lemon
small bunch of dill, chopped

Start to finish: 15 minutes prep
+ 1½ hours cooking

Serves: 4 + lots of leftovers

WONDERFUL *white sauce*

100g (7 tbsp) butter
100g (¾ cup) plain/all-purpose flour
1.2 litres (5 cups) milk
salt and pepper

Start to finish: 15 minutes

Makes: enough for 2 small lasagnes
or macaroni cheese or cauliflower
cheese (see method for freezing
instructions)

Lucy

Judging by the response on our blog and YouTube channel, some of you seem to find making white sauce fiddly. It needn't be. Promise. It is quick and perfect to make in bulk as it freezes well, meaning that the only thing standing between you and a lasagne, cauliflower cheese or macaroni cheese is a bit of defrosting. It is also a great way of using up milk that is about to go out of date.

Melt the butter in a saucepan. Add the flour and stir with a wooden spoon until you have a smooth yellow paste. The French call this a roux.

Take the pan off the heat. Add a splash of milk. Put back over the heat, stirring all the time. When all the milk is absorbed, add a little more, stirring all the time, until all that is absorbed too. And so on, until all the milk has been added. The key is to add milk slowly and stir quickly. You can swap between a spoon and a whisk, if you like. Milk should be added off the heat and the sauce stirred on it.

When all the milk has been used, the sauce needs to be cooked for a further 5 minutes, stirring all the while. This is to cook the floury taste out of it leaving you with a silky, smooth sauce. Season with salt and pepper. If it is lumpy, don't worry – if whisking fails, you can sieve it.

This recipe makes quite a lot of sauce, so freeze it in batches. It keeps well in the fridge, but should be covered with clingfilm/plastic wrap when hot to avoid a thick skin developing.

Recipe suggestions

Melt 100g (1 cup) Cheddar cheese into a portion of white sauce. Smother the Roasted Cauliflower, page 81 in it. Top with breadcrumbs and some grated Parmesan cheese and grill/broil or roast until golden and bubbly.

Stir in some lemon juice and chopped dill for an accompaniment to fish.

Stir in some Dijon mustard.

Substitute half the milk with wine or stock for a lighter sauce.

If you want to step the white sauce up a gear, then put ½ onion, 1 bay leaf, 10 black peppercorns and a few parsley stalks into a saucepan with the milk. Bring to the boil, remove from the heat and allow to infuse for 30 minutes. Strain into a jug before adding to the roux, as above. This will add even more flavour to the final dish.

FREEZE!

If you currently have to chip away stalagmites and stalactites to get to your frozen sausages, welcome to our world! If, on the other hand, your freezer is a filing cabinet of neatly labelled, dated and triple-wrapped fish fingers, then move along, there's nothing to see here. You do not need to read this, and frankly we're not sure we'd like you if we met you.

That's because we're jealous. We have aspirations. Dreams. We too want order where there is chaos; we want to know whether it's homemade chocolate ice cream we're defrosting, or chicken liver pâté.

And the thing is, it's not difficult. All it takes is a pen, maybe a label, knowing what the date is, and bam! You are eating something identifiable that you froze in living memory. Joy!

Freezer burn is your enemy Although it won't poison you, it will affect the flavour and texture of food. To avoid it, push air out of freezer bags. Use containers the right size for what you are freezing, so there isn't loads of air. If there is, make sure you have a layer of liquid at the top of the food – so the stew's sauce covers the meat or veg, for example. Frozen liquids increase in size by 10% so make sure there is room for expansion.

Full freezers are more efficient than half-full ones Even if you don't use it for much, it's still worth filling it to keep it working efficiently, as it's cheaper. Fill it with sliced bread that you can use for toast. Check out the frozen aisle in your supermarket and discover a world of fruit and vegetables, frozen in their nutritional prime and sold cheap (see Slack Mummy Soup page 68 for more details) and stock up to keep your freezer full.

Make a date! Use permanent markers on stickers to tell you what it is that you froze. And then date it. Most food can be kept for 6–9 months. And while you're labelling that food, why not portion it correctly? There's nothing more annoying than having to defrost enough tomato sauce for 6 when you only need enough for 2. Portion out, using little plastic bags and feel very smug.

Have a system It doesn't have to be complicated. In most freezers the bottom drawer is coldest, so put new things there so they freeze quickly, then move them up a drawer next time you go shopping and put new things in the bottom drawer. This means the top drawer will always be full of the stuff you need to use soonest. But you'll know that already, because of all those labels you made with dates. Yes? Yes? Are you still there…?

Stock up If you make loads of stock/bouillon then obviously freeze it. But more usefully (and I actually do this!) keep a large freezer bag in the freezer dedicated to stock making. Every time you have chicken, put the bones, etc. in the chicken stock bag (you could have a veggie and a beef stock bag too, if you were really showing off). When it's full, make a huge pot of stock, rather than making small ones more frequently.

Crumbs! So useful, so underrated. Every time you don't finish the heel of bread or some toast doesn't get eaten, whizz it up. Put it in the 'crumbs bag' in the freezer and then you have crumbs on tap. And what isn't improved by a delicious crunchy topping? Particularly a delicious crunchy cheesy topping. Mmm.

Good things to freeze Biscuit and cookie dough, pizza dough (after it's proven once and been knocked back), cakes (when baked and ideally without icing), bacon and sausages. Bananas freeze brilliantly (see page 147), as do tortillas and wraps, egg whites, milk, wine for stock/bouillon, butter, grated cheese, soups and tomato sauces.

Don't freeze Meat or fish that has been frozen before. Freezing food doesn't improve it, so if something is past its prime, or you don't fancy eating it, freezing it won't make it taste any better. Freezing doesn't kill bacteria. Don't freeze anything hot as this will increase the temperature in the freezer, affecting all other food. Bring food down to room temperature and then freeze.

Argh! There's a power cut and your freezer is off. Do you need to throw out your food? Apparently not. Keep the freezer door closed and food will remain frozen for a further 24 hours. If cleaning your freezer, your food will stay frozen outside the freezer for a couple of hours, giving you time to get rid of those stalactites.

meat-free masterpieces

Never happier than chomping on a rare steak, you might think we would find going meat-free difficult. In fact we love vegetables and there are loads more vegetarian recipes dotted throughout the book. Because although steak, and meat generally, is lovely, you don't want it all the time.

Which is lucky, because it's expensive! Organic, free-range and locally sourced are the buzzwords when it comes to meat and each word seems to add more to the cost, but they are words that can't be ignored. What price a happy pig/sheep/cow/chicken? We both eat the best-quality meat we can afford, from local butchers. And that means we don't eat it that often, which is fine! Because meanwhile there is Fantastic Falafel (see page 77). So delicious and easy it gives sausages a run for their money.

The other thing about veggie meals is that they are almost accidentally healthy. How can they not be when they are full of vegetables? Nobody's going to get lardy or nutrient deficient tucking into Ginger and Parsnip Soup (see page 70). In fact, the worst thing about eating veggie is the sense of worthiness that can creep over you, at odds with the deliciousness of the food. We can't say 'Chickpea Soup' without yawning, but the reality is far from dull (see opposite). Tortilla Tower (see page 78) tries a bit harder to entice, but it's made from haricot beans. That's right, pulses, but pulses fried with garlic and chilli, served with cheesy, floury tortillas, with guacamole on the side. Arriba, baby! So, if you needed persuading about going a bit meat-free, trust us on this one. Give any of these recipes a go. You'll never look back.

CHICKPEA soup

3 tbsp olive oil
1 large onion, chopped
3 big handfuls of baby leaf spinach
1 x 400g (14 oz) tin of chopped
    tomatoes
2 x 400g (14 oz) tins of chickpeas
450ml (2 scant cups) vegetable
    stock/bouillon
salt and pepper
2 tbsp extra-virgin olive oil
3 tbsp lemon juice

Start to finish: 10 minutes prep
+ 10 minutes cooking

Serves: 4

If your child will eat this, have a medal! But as we know, most won't. However, a family cookbook isn't all about kids. It's about you too. After rushing home from work on a Monday night, to bath and put them to bed, you deserve a big bowl of goodness. That's what this is, a healthy supper, made in minutes from ingredients you can get from your corner shop.

Splosh the olive oil into a large saucepan and put it on the heat. Once hot, throw in the onion and cook until it is soft and translucent. Add the spinach and tomatoes, cook for 1 minute and then add the well-rinsed chickpeas.

Add the stock, bring to the boil and simmer for 10 minutes. Season with salt and pepper. When ready to serve, splash in the extra-virgin olive oil and lemon juice.

Serving suggestions This is a Cypriot dish, often served with bread and feta cheese on the side or sprinkled on top, or tinned sardines.

150g (5 oz) frozen vegetables
enough water or stock/bouillon
   to cover
a generous dollop of cream
   cheese/crème fraîche/Greek
   yogurt – whatever you have in
   the fridge
chives or flat-leaf parsley, to garnish

Start to finish: 5 minutes

Serves: 1 child

SLACK mummy soup

When our children were very young and we worried their legs might turn into rickety breadsticks and their blood into hummus due to all the, ahem, 'mezze' style teas we'd given them, we'd make this. The trick is to always have a bag of frozen veg in the freezer. Frozen butternut squash is a winner, as is a winter vegetable mix, available from most supermarkets (just pick out some of the onion or leek if there's too much). It might not sound very exciting, but add cream cheese, or some other dairy product and you get a delicious cheesy, creamy mush that kids love.

Put the vegetables in a pan and cover with boiling water or stock/bouillon and cook for 4–5 minutes.

Once cooked, strain the vegetables, keeping a couple of tablespoons of the cooking liquid. Add as much cheese/yogurt as you think your child wants, and purée with a blender.

Serve with a swirl of cream cheese/crème fraîche/yogurt and garnish with the herbs. Hey presto! A meal for your child, which isn't hummus and breadsticks.

Frozen vegetables Until we had kids, infrequent visits to the frozen food aisle in a supermarket left us with the impression it was full of lurid desserts and elaborate ice cream. But more recent scourings – looking for things to make life a little easier on the food front – have shown us that the frozen aisle is chock-full of vegetables. Vegetables which have been picked in season and frozen within hours of being harvested, so maintaining a high vitamin content at the same time as being quite cheap.

Obviously peas are there, but we're guessing you've found the peas. However, there are lots more. We've mentioned a winter vegetable mix, full of carrots, swedes/rutabaga, chopped onions and leeks. But frozen peppers, green beans – whole or sliced, baby carrots, broccoli florets and broad/fava beans are all available. Which means no washing or chopping required – just pop into a pan of boiling water and simmer.

SUMMER BRUSCHETTA
with winter possibilities

2 slices rustic/country/sourdough
   bread
1 garlic clove, peeled
8 cherry tomatoes
freshly ground black pepper
sea salt
good-quality olive oil
a few torn basil leaves

Start to finish: 5 minutes

Serves: 1 (scale up as needed)

One of my many favourite ways to eat tomatoes is on bruschetta (pronounced brusketta). You need good ripe fruit, good olive oil and charred crusty bread.

Lightly toast the bread and rub one side with a peeled, raw garlic clove. The clove will disappear rapidly, as you are grating it on the roughness of the bread, imparting a gorgeous garlic flavour.

I always use cherry tomatoes because too often bigger varieties disappoint, whereas cherries provide a more reliable little burst of sweetness that I love. Quarter them and put them in a bowl with a good grind of pepper, some sea salt, a tablespoon of good quality olive oil and a few torn basil leaves. Mix thoroughly and then pour onto the bread. Drizzle a tiny bit more oil over the top and eat.

If you can't get any decent tomatoes, then follow the recipe on page 49 for roasting them and enjoy a wintry bruschetta instead.

GINGER AND PARSNIP soup

INGREDIENTS

50g (½ stick) butter
1 onion, sliced
a thumb-sized piece of ginger root,
   very finely sliced
800g (1¾ oz) parsnips, diced
1 tsp ground mixed spice/pumpkin
   pie spice
½ tsp ground cumin
zest of 1 lime
1 litre (1 quart) chicken stock/bouillon
salt and pepper
150ml (⅔ cup) cream of coconut
optional garnish: sweet smoked
   paprika and coriander/cilantro,
   finely chopped

Start to finish: 10 minutes prep
+ 50 minutes simmering

Serves: 4 with leftovers

Parsnip is a vegetable that scrubs up well. In the fridge's bottom drawer, it looks about as appealing as your legs in winter. But give it a blast of heat and the parsnip becomes a wondrous thing. This soup shows it at its best. Sweet and creamy, the coconut milk makes it almost exotic, and there's some underlying heat from the ginger. It's your legs, after a holiday to Thailand and a vat of fake tan.

Melt the butter in a large saucepan. Add the onion, ginger and parsnips and gently fry for 5 minutes. Add the mixed spice, cumin and lime zest to the pan and cook for 2 minutes. Add chicken stock, salt and pepper and bring to the boil. Then reduce the heat, cover the pan and simmer for 45 minutes or until the parsnips are tender.

Allow the soup to cool slightly, then purée with a hand-held blender until smooth. Season again if required. Add the cream of coconut and reheat gently, but don't let it boil as this will spoil the flavour. Serve dusted with the sweet smoked paprika and a sprinkling of coriander/cilantro.

GIANT COUSCOUS
and apple salad

Claire

I've just discovered giant couscous and am wondering where it has been all my life. Nubbly, tasty and easy to prepare, it gives a herby salad some ballast. This is a lovely, summery supper, served in a wrap with some hummus, griddled halloumi cheese and a glass of something cold and white. Alternatively, serve it as a side with chicken or fish. The fragrance of the greenery might mean your kids don't reject it as quickly as they do any other salad item. I emphasise 'might'.

Put the onion and garlic into a cup with half the lemon juice. This reduces the strength of their flavours, which means you won't still be tasting onion and garlic the next day.

Bring the stock to the boil in a medium-sized saucepan. Then add the couscous and simmer for 6–8 minutes (or follow the packet instructions).

While it's bubbling away, finely chop the parsley and mint. Put it in a large bowl.

Toast the cumin and cinnamon in a dry frying pan over a medium heat until it darkens slightly and you can smell the aroma. Add it to the herbs.

Put the almonds in the same pan and toast briefly, stirring occasionally until they are a slightly darker brown. Add to the bowl. Grate the ginger straight into the bowl.

Chop the apple, throw in the bowl and then add the remaining lemon juice. Toss well and season with salt and pepper. Drain the couscous thoroughly and add to the salad bowl.

Drain the onion and garlic and add to the salad. Stir in the pomegranate molasses, if using, if not, a drizzle of honey.

INGREDIENTS

½ red onion, finely chopped
1 garlic clove, finely chopped
juice of 1 lemon
450ml (1 cup) chicken stock/bouillon
100g (⅔ cup) giant couscous, or normal couscous
small bunch of flat-leaf parsley
small bunch of mint
1 tsp ground cumin
1 tsp ground cinnamon
handful of unblanched whole almonds
1 tsp fresh ginger root, grated
1 apple, chopped
salt and pepper
1 tbsp pomegranate molasses (optional), or a drizzle of honey

Start to finish: 20 minutes prep

Serves: 2 as a main, 4 as a side

AUBERGINE, RED PEPPER
and fennel seed stew

6 tbsp olive oil
1 red onion, sliced
2 red peppers, sliced
3 garlic cloves, crushed
1 large aubergine/eggplant, cubed
1 tbsp fennel seeds
1 tsp dried oregano
3 red chilli peppers, deseeded and
    finely chopped
400ml (1¾ cups) passata/tomato
    sauce
2 tbsp tomato purée/paste
salt and pepper
crusty bread and feta cheese,
    to serve

Start to finish: 15 minutes prep
+ 1 hour cooking

Serves: 4

I have been making this for as long as I can remember. It is a soothing supper that is perfect for a mid-week dinner, but with some sprucing up can easily impress veggie dinner guests. It is also a good one to serve committed carnivores, as aubergine/eggplant is quite a meaty vegetable.

Heat the olive oil in a large frying pan and fry the onion, peppers and garlic until they soften.

Add the aubergine and continue to fry until it is soft too. Then add the fennel seeds, oregano and chillies. It should smell heavenly. Stir and cook for a couple of minutes, before adding the passata/tomato sauce and tomato purée/paste.

Bring to the boil, then reduce the heat. Cook on a low heat for about an hour until the sauce is thick and rich. Season with salt and pepper.

Serve with crusty bread and some feta cheese crumbled on top.

Lucy

Claire

SPANAKOPITA

What a mouthful! But so much better to tell your child they are having spanakopita for lunch, than spinach pie. My kids love spanakopita, but retch at the thought of spinach. The two things occupy totally different parts of their brain. It's amazing what the addition of feta cheese, fragrant herbs and some crispy filo/phyllo pastry can do. This is a great make-ahead weekend lunch or supper and perfect for a summer picnic.

Preheat the oven to 160°C/325°F/gas mark 3.

Fry the spring onions/scallions in a large frying pan with about 3 tbsp of olive oil.

Make sure the spinach is defrosted and well-drained. I put it in a sieve and squeeze it with a spoon to make sure all the water is out.

Once the spring onions are translucent, add the spinach and season lightly with salt and pepper. Fry for another 5 minutes or so.

Place the chopped herbs in a large bowl, and add the crumbled feta – it doesn't have to be uniformly crumbled; it's a bit more interesting if it isn't. Season with pepper and stir the fried spinach in.

Grease an ovenproof dish. I use a 25 x 32cm (10 x 12 inch) ceramic one, and using a pastry brush, paint with a mixture of the melted butter and a splash of olive oil.

Take a sheet of filo/phyllo pastry and place on the bottom of the dish, folding in any ends which may be too long. Paint with the butter/oil mix, and place the next sheet of pastry on top; do the same thing, and then place the third pastry sheet on top. Spread the spinach mix evenly over the pastry, then place the remaining pastry sheets on top, using the same method of painting with butter/oil. Cut into portions.

Pop in the oven and bake for 50 minutes, until the top is golden brown. Serve hot or cold.

INGREDIENTS

bunch of spring onions/scallions, finely chopped
olive oil
300g (10 oz) frozen spinach, defrosted and well-drained
3 tbsp finely chopped mint
3 tbsp finely chopped dill
200g (7 oz) feta cheese, crumbled
70g (5 tbsp) butter, melted and allowed to cool
1 packet ready-made filo pastry/phyllo dough, around 270g (9½ oz)
salt and pepper

Start to finish: 20 minutes prep + 50 minutes in the oven

Serves: 4

LEEK AND POTATO
pie with a cheddar crust

1 x 320g (11½ oz) packet of ready-
rolled all-butter puff pastry
100g (3½ oz) potatoes, peeled and
chopped quite small
1 leek, thinly sliced
knob of butter
50g (1 scant cup) mushroom, sliced
small bunch of thyme
1 tbsp cream cheese
30g (⅓ cup) grated Cheddar cheese
salt and pepper
1 egg beaten, or some milk to give
the pastry a sheen

Start to finish: 15 minutes prep
 + 12–15 minutes in the oven

Makes: 2 pies

Who doesn't love a pie, especially one with a Cheddar crust – ooh, get us! Here we've suggested a potato and leek filling, but that buttery, crunchy pastry is the perfect foil for any medley of leftovers in your fridge. There's something about individual pies which both kids and grown-ups love.

Take the puff pastry out of the fridge 10 minutes before you want to use it.

Pop the potatoes in a pan of cold water. Bring to the boil and let simmer for 10 minutes.

Fry the leek in a frying pan with the butter. Add the mushrooms and thyme leaves to the leeks. Fry for about 5 minutes until the leek is translucent.

Drain the potatoes and put them in the pan with the leeks and mushrooms. Stir in the cream cheese and the grated Cheddar. Season well.

Preheat the oven to 220°C/425°F/gas mark 7.

Unroll the pastry and cut two circles, one at each end of the pastry, leaving as much pastry intact in the middle as possible. Each circle should be 15cm (6 inches) in diameter (I use a saucepan lid).

Next, make the Cheddar crust – this bit is optional, as making the Cheddar crust is a faff! But if you have the time/inclination, it's a nice addition (see panel on the left for instructions). If not, just go straight to the next step.

Making the Cheddar crust (optional) Grate a handful of cheese over half the intact pastry. Fold the other half over it and with a rolling pin, roll the pastry together, until it is about 3mm (⅛ inch) thick.

Using a slightly smaller circle, maybe a saucer, cut two more circles. These are the lids of the pie.

Place half the filling on each 15cm (6 inch) piece of pastry, leaving a space of at least 1.5cm (¾ inch) around the edge. Using a pastry brush, paint milk or egg around the edge of the circle. Place the lid on top of the filling and using your fingertips push the bottom edge to the lid's edge. If the lid and the base don't quite meet, remove some of the filling.

Once the pie is sealed, give it a wash with the milk/egg and using a knife, make a slit in the pastry lid to let steam out. Put the pies on a lined baking tray and pop in the oven for 12 –15 minutes. They are ready when the pastry is golden brown.

FANTASTIC *falafel*

INGREDIENTS

2 x 400g (14 oz) tins of chickpeas
1 large onion, finely chopped (or use
    frozen ready-chopped)
2 garlic cloves, crushed
small bunch of flat-leaf parsley,
    chopped
2 tsp ground cumin
2 tsp ground coriander
1 tsp harissa (optional)
4 tbsp plain/all-purpose flour
salt
vegetable oil

To serve
wraps or pitta bread
hummus
harissa
gherkins
sliced tomatoes
shredded cabbage

Start to finish: 5 minutes prep
+ 10–15 minutes cooking

Serves: 4

Little nuggets of deliciousness, stuffed in a wrap, covered in hummus and sprinkled with vegetables (well, we can but try). We first started eating this at a little Lebanese cafe. Now we've discovered how easy it is to cook it ourselves, we eat falafel all the time. If your kids are dubious, tell them it's hummus chips, as the ingredients are virtually identical.

Rinse the chickpeas well and drain. Place in a bowl with the onion, garlic, parsley, cumin, coriander, harissa (if using), flour and some salt. Then using a hand-held blender, food processor or – if you're feeling strong – potato masher, whizz the ingredients into a paste.

Use damp hands to shape spoonfuls of the mix into small patties and place on a plate, ready to cook.

Heat enough vegetable oil to cover the base of a large frying pan. Once the oil is hot (it should sizzle when you put something in it), place the patties in the pan – they shouldn't touch each other, so you will probably have to cook several batches.

After 2–3 minutes they should be golden on one side. Turn them with a spatula and let them cook for another couple of minutes.

Serve in a wrap that has been smeared with hummus and harissa, and loaded with gherkins, sliced tomatoes and shredded cabbage.

Cooking like clockwork When cooking small patties or fritters, it's a good idea to try and remember which patty you put in the pan first, as that will obviously be the first cooked. One way of doing this is to think of a clock's face. Put the first patty in at 12 o'clock and work your way round. When it's time to turn the patties, or take them out of the pan, start there. Another good thing to remember is that as you cook the second or third batches of patties, the oil and the pan are hotter. You don't want the patties' outsides to scorch and the insides to be uncooked, so turn the heat down a little with each new batch.

TORTILLA *tower*

Refried beans
a large glug of olive oil
2 medium onions, chopped
2 garlic cloves, chopped
stalks from a small bunch of
    coriander/cilantro
½ tsp dried chilli flakes
3 x 400g (14 oz) tins of haricot/navy
    beans, rinsed and drained
salt and pepper
200ml (scant 1 cup) crème fraîche
juice of ½ lime

Salsa
1 x 400g (14 oz) tin of chopped
    tomatoes
leaves from a small bunch of
    coriander/cilantro
juice of ½ lime
1 small onion, chopped
salt and pepper
½ teaspoon dried chilli flakes
    (optional)

Topping
olive oil
1 small onion, finely chopped
3 big or 5 medium-sized flour tortillas
200g (1½ cups) grated Cheddar
    cheese

Guacamole
1 avocado
black pepper
squeeze of lime juice

Start to finish: 30 minutes
+ 15 minutes in the oven

Serves: 4

We loathe long ingredients lists too. Who has the time to read them, let alone go out and buy it all? This ingredients list might look overwhelming, but on closer examination you'll see you've already got most of it in the cupboard. Just buy some coriander/cilantro on your way home from work, and knock it up for a delicious Friday night supper. Alternatively have it as a Saturday night dinner with the kids; they'll love it too.

First, cook the beans: heat the oil in a large pan. Add the onions and fry until soft and translucent. Add the garlic and fry for another 2 minutes, until it starts to brown. Add coriander/cilantro stalks and chilli flakes and fry for another 2 minutes. Add the beans and continue to fry over a low heat. This step takes about 10–15 minutes; you want the beans to lose their shape and have a porridge-like consistency. Season with salt and pepper. Take off the heat and stir in the crème fraîche and lime juice.

To make the salsa, strain some of the juice from the chopped tomatoes; you don't want them too sloppy. Put the tomatoes, coriander, lime juice and onion in a bowl. Stir and season with salt and pepper. Add chilli flakes, to taste, if you want. Stir the salsa into the refried beans.

Preheat the oven to 200°C/400°F/gas mark 6.

To make the onion topping for the tower, heat some olive oil in a small frying pan and throw in the finely chopped onion. Fry gently until the onions have softened and become translucent.

While they are cooking you can make the tower. Lay the first tortilla in a baking pan or ovenproof dish. Spread a layer of the refried beans mix over it; it should be about 2–3cm (about 1 inch) deep, sprinkle over a layer of cheese and place a tortilla on top. Keep doing this until you have used up the refried beans mixture and most of the cheese and have got to the last tortilla. Place the last tortilla on the top, sprinkle over the remaining cheese and scatter the fried onion over the top. Bake for 10–15 minutes.

While it's in the oven, mash up the avocado, season with pepper and sprinkle with lime juice.

Take the tower out of the oven when the cheese is golden and melted on top. Serve with guacamole on the side.

Refried beans – it's true love Sad but true. Refried beans are AWESOME. Not in a 'they're quick and easy and I have all the ingredients in my cupboard' kind of way. But in a 'oooh, what shall I have for dinner tonight? I know! Refried beans. I really, really want refried beans' kind of way.

Admittedly their name doesn't do them any favours. It's from the Mexican dish, frijoles refritos, which actually means 'well-fried beans' as they are fried within an inch of their life. And we all know anything fried has loads of flavour. We used haricot/navy beans in this recipe, but you could try it with any beans you have in your cupboard.

Rinsing beans You should rinse tinned beans really well, until the water stops frothing. This will get rid of the starch which can have a, you know, lively effect on your insides. Nuff said!

If you can't be bothered with the faffing in this recipe, don't worry. Just make the refried beans bit and serve in wraps, with guacamole, sour cream and a soft-boiled egg. No one will judge you. They'll be too busy shovelling it down.

sides

Sides are having a moment. Do you remember when a side was essentially potatoes, a bit of rice and maybe some boiled green beans? Not any more. Side dishes have become show stealers in their own right and sometimes we are so obsessed with them – and yes Roast Cauliflower (see opposite), we mean you! – we don't even bother with the mains.

Most of the recipes in this chapter are easy to make. Butter Bean Mash (see page 85), is essentially a tin of butter beans, mashed and seasoned well with lemon and olive oil. Perfect for those nights when you crave something spud-like, but can't be bothered with the peeling. And as for Cavolo Nero with Lemon and Garlic (see page 84), if you were a man we would marry you. Just think how beautiful our children would be.

We are constantly being told we should eat more vegetables and this chapter just made that a whole lot easier.

ROAST *cauliflower*

1 cauliflower
olive oil
salt and pepper

Start to finish: 2 minutes prep
+ 30 minutes cooking time

Serves: 4

For ages we were stuck in a vegetable rut. Carrots were sliced and boiled, peppers chopped and roasted, courgettes/zucchini ribboned and fried. Cauliflower was only ever eaten after bubbling away in a saucepan for a good 5 minutes, and always served with cheese sauce. Last year, on a trip to Tel Aviv, we had it roasted. It was a revelation… like discovering a new exotic vegetable. Charred, crispy and full of flavour, we have never cooked it any other way since.

Preheat the oven to 180°C/350°F/gas mark 4.

Wash the cauliflower and separate into florets. The easiest way is to turn the cauliflower on its head, cut out the stalk with a paring knife and then chop off individual florets at the base of their trunks.

Put the florets in a roasting tin – making sure the pieces are not too close together as you want the cauliflower to roast, not steam – and coat thoroughly with olive oil. Season generously with salt and pepper. Cook for about 30 minutes until the florets are lightly charred. Don't be scared of the edges going brown – it just makes them tastier.

CREAMY LEEKS
with parmesan breadcrumbs

INGREDIENTS

2 leeks or 8 baby leeks, sliced
100ml (scant ½ cup) chicken or
  vegetable stock/bouillon
1 tbsp cream cheese (plain, or
  with garlic and herbs)
salt and pepper
1 tbsp finely grated Parmesan
  cheese
1 tbsp breadcrumbs

Start to finish: 10 minutes

Serves: 4

Cream cheese is a remarkably versatile ingredient and one that is always good to have in your fridge. Don't bother with the branded stuff, the supermarket's own-label is half the price and just as good. Here, the cheese is stirred through some lightly poached leeks, sprinkled with Parmesan breadcrumbs and grilled/broiled.

In a small saucepan, cook the leeks in the stock/bouillon until they are tender. Drain and mix in the cream cheese. Season with salt and pepper. Put in a small gratin dish. Mix together the Parmesan and breadcrumbs and sprinkle over the top.

Blitz under a hot grill/broiler. This is delicious as a side dish or served alongside chicken or pork.

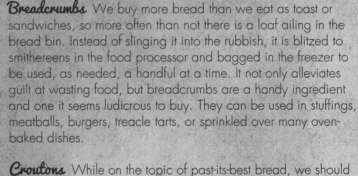

Breadcrumbs We buy more bread than we eat as toast or sandwiches, so more often than not there is a loaf ailing in the bread bin. Instead of slinging it into the rubbish, it is blitzed to smithereens in the food processor and bagged in the freezer to be used, as needed, a handful at a time. It not only alleviates guilt at wasting food, but breadcrumbs are a handy ingredient and one it seems ludicrous to buy. They can be used in stuffings, meatballs, burgers, treacle tarts, or sprinkled over many oven-baked dishes.

Croutons While on the topic of past-its-best bread, we should talk croutons. Easy to make, you just cut the bread into squares, including crusts if you want the more rustic look. Bake in a hot oven – about 200°C/400°F/gas mark 6 – drizzled with lots of olive oil (garlic-infused oil rings a nice change) and salt and pepper until they are golden. This takes between 5–10 minutes, depending on the bread you are using and the size of your croutons. They need turning once. They keep for ages in an airtight plastic container, and are a great way of pepping up a smooth soup or a salad.

UNCLE BREND'S *apple slaw*

INGREDIENTS

½ red cabbage
2 carrots (you don't need to peel)
4 spring onions/scallions
2 tbsp olive oil
2 tbsp cider vinegar
juice of 1 lime
2 tbsp runny honey
2 apples (again, it's not necessary
   to peel)
salt and pepper

Start to finish: 15 minutes

Serves: 4

Uncle Brendan is a bit of a saint. Not only is he adored by Claire's two unruly boys, he makes a mean cup of coffee in the morning AND does the washing up. He also cooks. He likes to keep it healthy, and his meticulous nature means he usually chops everything up really small. This is just what you want in a coleslaw. This one is sweet and delicious, and tastes even better the next day when the flavours have all had the chance to get to know each other and mingle.

Grate the cabbage into a large bowl – you could use a food processor or a hand-held grater. Next, grate the carrots into the cabbage. Now finely slice the spring onions/scallions and add to the mix.

Make the dressing. Combine the olive oil, cider vinegar, lime juice, honey, and salt and pepper in a small bowl. Whisk together the ingredients with a fork, then pour over the slaw mix.

Slice the apples into thin matchsticks and add to the dressed slaw, mix immediately. Toss together all the ingredients, then cover and place in the fridge to be served chilled. Nice with pink pancakes (page 126).

ROOT VEGETABLE *gratin*

INGREDIENTS

300ml (1¼ cups) single/light cream
300ml (1¼ cups) milk
2 sprigs of rosemary
3 garlic cloves, crushed
2 parsnips, peeled
2 carrots, peeled
500g (18 oz) Maris Piper (Yukon
   Gold or Russet) potatoes, peeled
salt and pepper
handful of Parmesan cheese
handful of breadcrumbs

Start to finish: 15 minutes prep
+ 1 hour cooking

Serves: 6 (or 4 as a main)

This creamy gratin is indulgent, but it's also a really great way to eat vegetables. Delicious with a roast or a pie, or on its own with greens or a salad on the side, it's an easy, cheap and healthy dinner – well, only if you ignore all the cream!

Put the cream, milk and rosemary in a small saucepan over a low heat and warm without boiling. Take off the heat and add the crushed garlic. Using a food processor or mandolin (pay attention, if you don't want to lose a finger) or sharp knife, finely slice the vegetables. They should be about 3-mm (⅛-inch) thick.

Preheat the oven to 200°C/400°F/gas mark 6.

In a baking dish, arrange each vegetable in a layer. We like layering carrots, potatoes, parsnips (which are the star of this dish incidentally), seasoning each layer with salt and pepper. Fish out the rosemary sprig and pour over the milk and cream mixture. It should just about cover the top layer, but not swamp it.

Cover with foil and bake for 30–40 minutes. Uncover and sprinkle with the Parmesan cheese and breadcrumbs. Bake for a further 20 minutes until golden brown, but most importantly until all the vegetables are completely tender.

SWEET POTATO WEDGES
with smoked paprika dip

INGREDIENTS

750g (26 oz) sweet potatoes
50ml (scant ¼ cup) olive oil
sea salt and pepper

Dip
250g (1 heaping cup)
    mayonnaise
1 tbsp smoked paprika

Start to finish: 5 minutes prep
+ 35–40 minutes in the oven

Serves: 4

Forget shop-bought oven chips or fries with their expense and lack of nutrition. Embrace the sweet potato wedge instead. Almost as easy (honest!) as the potatoes don't need to be peeled; just hurriedly chopped. Hurrah! And much, much better for you with all that beta-carotene. Plus, crucially, they are DELICIOUS.

Preheat the oven to 200°C/400°F/gas mark 6.

Cut your sweet potatoes into chips. Think chunky, gastro-pub size, rather than skinny fries. Leave the skins on.

Place them on a baking sheet and season with salt and pepper. Go as heavy as you like on the pepper, as it mellows out in cooking. Pour over the olive oil and toss with your hands until all the potatoes are coated. Make sure there is a bit of space between each chip so that they roast, rather than steam. Bake in the oven for 35–40 minutes until brown. Take out and flip over halfway through.

To make the dip, just mix the mayonnaise and smoked paprika in a small bowl.

CAVOLO NERO
with lemon and garlic

INGREDIENTS

1kg (2¼ lb) cavolo nero
    (it reduces considerably)
olive oil
juice of 1 lemon
1 garlic clove, crushed
salt and pepper

Start to finish: 5 minutes

Serves: 4

Serving tip Delicious on toast for a quick and healthy lunch, good in minestrone-like soups and as a side to roasts, pies and stews.

This leafy brassica was our food discovery of last year and is now our favourite vegetable of all time. It is also rather sweetly called dinosaur cabbage, although its name actually means black cabbage in Italian. It has a pleasantly tangy, bitter flavour, with a sweet aftertaste, and you can practically feel each mouthful boosting your immune system and giving you muscles like Popeye. It doesn't form a head like most cabbages, so it comes in bags of dark green, almost black, palm-frond like leaves. Smaller ones are more tender. Avoid leaves with holes in them. This recipe comes from London's best greengrocer, Andreas of Chelsea.

Cut out the woody stalk of each leaf, and then cut the leaves into strips. Steam the leaves over a pan of simmering water for 3 minutes until lightly wilted. Meanwhile, heat a little oil in a large frying pan. When hot, fry the garlic briefly. Stir it well, so it doesn't catch (burnt garlic is nasty and bitter). Then add the leaves, squeeze in the lemon juice and cook for 2 minutes.

200g (7 oz) swede/rutabaga, peeled and chopped
200g (7 oz) carrots, peeled and chopped
large knob of butter
freshly ground black pepper
100g (1 cup) strong Cheddar cheese, grated

Start to finish: 10 minutes prep + 15–30 minutes in the oven

Serves: 4–6

GREENWICH *bake*

We first ate this at our cousin John's house in London's Greenwich – hence the name – and have been cooking it regularly ever since. Quite simply it is swede/rutabaga and carrot mashed with loads of black pepper and butter, topped with cheese and grilled/broiled. It is sweet, but savoury and great with a roast, a meat pie or sausages and gravy.

Preheat the grill/broiler to hot.

Steam or boil the vegetables until they are tender. Mash them with the butter and lots of black pepper.

While still hot, put them in a square 20-cm (8-inch) ovenproof dish. Scatter the cheese over the top and place under the hot grill/broiler until the cheese has melted.

Cheat's tip Swede and carrots can often be bought ready peeled and chopped at many supermarkets, so cheat if you want to.

40ml (3 scant tbsp) garlic-infused olive oil (or olive oil and 1 crushed garlic clove, added with the lemon zest)
zest of 1 unwaxed lemon
2 x 400g (14 oz) tins of butter beans/lima beans, drained
salt and pepper

Start to finish: 5 minutes

Serves: 4

BUTTER BEAN *mash*

This is so tasty it is hard to believe it only takes 5 minutes to make. It is the perfect solution to those nights when you feel like something warm and comforting like mashed potato, but can't be bothered to do any peeling.

Heat the garlic-infused oil in a saucepan, add the lemon zest and cook it slowly for a minute or two on a low heat. You want the oil to take on the lemon flavour.

Add the beans to the pan and stir so they are nicely coated. When warmed through, take a potato masher and ever so lightly mash the beans. You don't want them smooth, but you don't want them whole, either. Somewhere in between. Season to taste.

Lucy

SPROUTS

Sprouts. There is, I suppose, something dire in the sound, and then there's the reputation: soggy balls of gunk that blighted many a childhood and still cast a greenish shadow over Christmas feasts. It is possible sprouts are the most disliked and derided of all vegetables.

This saddens and confuses me in equal measure. We are all familiar with craving certain foods. I mean non-pregnant craving for foods that at certain times manage to feed more than just hunger: curry, fish and chips, sushi, a steaming bowl of pho. For me, sprouts cooked properly slot comfortably into this lofty company and I promise that, however entrenched your dislike, knocking up this dish will force a revision of your revulsion.

First, catch your sprouts. A good handful each is enough as a side dish. Forget about scoring a cross across the bottom, it's unnecessary. Pull off the mankiest outer leaves and give them a rinse.

Next, sling the lot into a pan of boiling, salted water. DO NOT STEAM! No matter what celebrity chefs may tell you. Take it from a sproutophile.

Next the trimmings, by which I mean smoked streaky bacon. Chop it and fry it in a pan with a smidgen of olive oil over a medium heat until crispy. Check your sprouts. They're probably not ready yet but better safe than sorry. About 7 minutes or so should do it.

Meanwhile, open a packet of ready-cooked chestnuts and chop them. Again, quantities are personal, but about half as much volume as the sprouts is good. Chuck them in with the bacon and stir.

As soon as the sprouts are ready, drain them and throw them into the bacon/chestnut pan. Mix, season (although remember salt is already present from the bacon) and serve.

INGREDIENTS

400g (14 oz) Brussels sprouts
olive oil
8 rashers/slices of smoked streaky
    bacon, chopped
200g (7 oz) ready-cooked and
    peeled chestnuts (most come
    vacuum packed)
freshly ground black pepper

Start to finish: 10 minutes

Serves: 4

PEA AND FETA *salad*

INGREDIENTS

450g (1 lb) frozen petit pois or
    garden peas
6 spring onions/scallions, finely
    sliced
small bunch of mint, finely chopped
zest of 1 lime
juice of ¼ lemon
2 tbsp virgin olive oil
75g (3 oz) feta cheese
freshly ground black pepper

Start to finish: 10 minutes

Serves: 4

Despite hating most forms of salad, lots of kids love this one. Partly it's the salty feta cheese, partly it's the zingy lime zest, but mostly it's the peas. Sweet, delicious and permanently available in the freezer, this is a side dish you can always knock together in no time. Great for days when you can't remember the last time they ate something green.

Bring a medium pan of water to the boil. Throw in the peas and let them cook for about 4 minutes, drain in a colander and place under cold running water (this helps them to keep their bright green colour).

Put the drained peas in a bowl along with the spring onions/scallions, mint, lime zest, lemon juice and olive oil. Crumble in the feta cheese, season with pepper and toss.

CHAPTER 7

one-pot stop

Life sometimes feels too short to be stacking dishwashers and with these one-pot wonders you won't have to. The hard work is done in just one pan, meaning there is very little washing up. Hurrah! This leaves you with plenty of time to write that novel, paint your nails or watch back-to-back episodes of your favourite soap.

It is not just stews that are our saviour here. Shake and Bake (chicken pieces, shaken in a marinade and baked with sausages, potato wedges and onions, see page 93), Mr Plowman's Fish Stew (see page 100) and our homemade British Baked Beans (see opposite) – their speed and flavour counter their infamous side effects – are all regular family favourites in the Crumbs' households. This all means that you will never have to cook with two pots again, and that's a copper-bottomed (pan) promise.

TOMATO-CHORIZO
no-stir risotto

INGREDIENTS

1 onion, finely chopped
25g (2 tbsp) butter
75g (3 oz) chorizo, sliced into half
   moons
250g (1¼ cups) arborio rice
800ml (scant 3½ cups) chicken
   stock/bouillon
250ml (1 cup) passata/tomato
   sauce
sprig of thyme
small tin of sweetcorn/corn kernels
Parmesan cheese and garlic bread,
   to serve

Start to finish: 10 minutes prep
+ 20 minutes cooking

Serves: 4

This is quick and simple and works well for both the children's teatime and your dinner. We eat ours with garlic bread and lots of grated Parmesan cheese. Leftovers are delicious, made into patties fried in olive oil and topped with more Parmesan.

In a large-ish saucepan, fry the onion in the butter until it is soft. Add the chorizo and cook for a minute or so. Add the rice and stir for another minute, until it is coated in butter. Add the stock, passata/tomato sauce and thyme and bring to the boil.

Give it a good stir, turn the heat down to a simmer, and clamp a lid on for 15–20 minutes. It is ready when the rice is cooked and all the liquid is absorbed. Fish out the thyme sprig and stir through a tin of sweetcorn/corn kernels until heated through.

Serve with Parmesan cheese and garlic bread.

BRITISH *baked beans*

INGREDIENTS

olive oil
1 bag soffrito (or one onion, two
   carrots, two celery sticks,
   chopped)
about 100g (3½ oz) pancetta,
   chopped
2 garlic cloves, crushed
2 x 400g (14 oz) tins of chopped
   tomatoes
pinch of dried chilli flakes
Worcestershire sauce
2 tsp English mustard
2 x 400g (14oz) tins of haricot/navy
   beans (or baked beans)
toast, to serve (optional)
Cheddar cheese (optional)
flat-leaf parsley (optional)
salt and pepper

Start to finish: 15 minutes prep
+ 50 minutes cooking

Serves: 4

Where would we be without baked beans? Countries have been built on them, wars won and at Crumbs, we are a bit of a fan. Although the beans that come in tins are magnificent, these, cooked with pancetta and tomatoes, trump anything else.

Put a drizzle of olive oil into a saucepan and place over a medium heat. Add the soffrito and pancetta. Cook until the vegetables are soft and then add the garlic. Once the pancetta is crispy, add the chopped tomatoes, chilli flakes and salt and pepper. Add a dash of Worcestershire sauce and the English mustard. Leave to cook on a low heat for about 30 minutes.

Rinse the beans. Once the sauce is rich and reduced, add the beans, mix and cook for a further 5–10 minutes. Season again to taste.

Serve on toast, in bowls with some grated cheese and chopped parsley or cold from the pan. This is great to take to school or work the next day either cold or heated up in the microwave.

Claire

OOH LA LA
sausage and lentil stew

This rustic casserole feels like a French take on sausages and mash. Slightly more sophisticated and a little bit healthier (it's those lentils), all the hard work is done at the beginning which means by dinnertime, all the chopping and frying is a distant memory. Other advantages over bangers and mash are you can make it in advance and reheat it. Plus, it freezes. What more could you ask?

Put a glug of oil in a large saucepan with a lid. Once the oil is hot, add the sausages and bacon, browning the sausages on all sides. This takes about 10 minutes. Don't skimp on the browning. There is nothing more unappetising – looking or tasting – than a flaccid sausage. Remove the sausages from the pan.

Put the onions in and a pinch of salt to stop them from burning. Cook until they become translucent.

If there is a lot of brown sausage fat on the bottom of the pan, chuck in a splash of red wine or stock, and scrape with a spatula to 'deglaze' the pan and keep the yummy flavours in the sauce.

Add the garlic, celery, carrot, pepper and lentils. Give them a stir, and then pour in the chicken stock/bouillon. Add the rosemary, thyme and browned sausages.

Bring to the boil, then cover and turn the heat down. Let it simmer for 25 minutes, until the lentils are cooked properly. Season with salt, pepper and a glug of balsamic vinegar. Serve with crusty bread and a green leaf salad.

INGREDIENTS

a glug of olive oil
12 pork sausages – nice chunky ones, not chipolatas
100g (4 oz) unsmoked bacon
2 red onions, roughly chopped
2 garlic cloves, cracked under the flat side of a knife
1 celery stick, sliced
1 carrot, sliced
½ red pepper, chopped
300g (1½ cups) dried Puy lentils
850ml (3½ cups) chicken stock/ bouillon
2 sprigs of rosemary
handful of thyme leaves
1 tbsp balsamic vinegar
salt and pepper

Start to finish: 20 minutes prep + 45 minutes cooking

Serves: 6

Freezing Simply cool this down, then pop it into a freezer bag, label and freeze.

LAMB AND ROSEMARY
one pot

1kg (2¼ lb) shoulder of lamb, chopped into small chunks
2 onions, sliced
1 tsp dried oregano
sprig of rosemary
2 tbsp olive oil
1 x 400g (14 oz) tin of chopped tomatoes
1 litre (1 quart) hot chicken stock/ bouillon
salt and pepper
crumbled feta cheese and crusty bread, to serve

Start to finish: 10 minutes prep + 2½ hours cooking time

Serves: 6

Lucy

Last winter I got into the habit of cooking a stew on a Saturday morning, to eat later in the week. It is a pleasant ritual. The children watch TV while I potter in my pyjamas, chopping onions, picking rosemary, opening tins of tomatoes and stirring in sprinkles of oregano. It is a very low-key and satisfying way to kick off the weekend. The ten-minute preparation time, minimal amount of washing up and freezability makes this one-pot wonder a household favourite.

Preheat the oven to 180°C/350°F/gas mark 4.

Put the lamb, onions, oregano, rosemary and olive oil into a large, wide casserole dish. Season, stir well, and bake uncovered for 45 minutes, stirring halfway through. (You can fry the meat first if you have time – it's more flavoursome – but it's fine just to pop everything in the dish at the same time if you prefer.)

Pour over the chopped tomatoes and stock, cover tightly with either a lid or aluminium foil, then return to the oven for 1½–2 hours, until the lamb is tender and the sauce thickened.

If you wish, stir some orzo or super-small pasta through 20 minutes before serving. Sprinkle with feta cheese and eat with crusty bread.

Grow rosemary! As a committed herb murderer, I am not one to give advice on horticulture. People say you need to be careful with mint as it can take over your garden – mine is a single crispy twig in the earth. But rosemary is different. Rosemary is impossible to kill.

Stick it in a pot on the windowsill, or in a lacklustre bit of your garden, and watch it take hold. Its woody branches get thicker, its leaves get bushier, you have a herb to be proud of. And once you've got it, most dishes can be improved. Shove it in the oven with vegetables you are roasting, and let the warm woody aroma fill your kitchen. Or blitz it up with sea salt in the food processor – one-third rosemary leaves to two-thirds salt. Voila! Rosemary salt to add flavour and sophistication to pork chops, roast potatoes and fries.

SHAKE and bake

INGREDIENTS

4 chicken thighs
8 sausages
4 potatoes, don't peel,
    just cut into wedges
2 onions, peeled and cut
    into wedges
olive oil
head of garlic
sprigs of rosemary or thyme
salt and pepper

Start to finish: 10 minutes prep
+ 50 minutes in the oven

Serves: 4

Sometimes after a day at the office or on the front line of childcare, we don't even have the energy to uncork a bottle of wine (thank goodness for screwtops!), let alone cook. This is when Shake and Bake comes into its own. All you do is toss some chicken pieces, sausages, onions and potato chunks (unpeeled!) into a roasting tin with olive oil, garlic and herbs. Shake it and then bake it in the oven. Yes, it really is that simple.

Preheat the oven to 180°C/350°F/gas mark 4.

You may need two roasting tins for this dish. You want the ingredients to have room to wiggle, so they roast and crisp up, instead of steaming, which they do if they are jostling for space.

Put the chicken, sausages, potato wedges and onion pieces into the roasting tin and toss thoroughly with olive oil. Pop in the head of garlic. If you need to divide it into cloves (i.e. if you are using two pans), then pop them in halfway through cooking, otherwise they will burn. Add the rosemary or thyme. Season with salt and pepper and bake for about 50 minutes, or until crispy and cooked through.

Variations Add chopped red or yellow peppers; use spare ribs or chicken drumsticks; add some lemon wedges; replace spuds with sweet potatoes.

SALMON
with artichokes and anchovies

INGREDIENTS

250g (9 oz) new potatoes – those little ready-washed ones are easiest
vegetable oil
2 salmon fillets
2 artichoke hearts from a tin, cut in half
2 anchovy fillets
juice of ½ lemon
a splosh of dry white wine
small bunch of flat-leaf parsley, chopped
salt and pepper

Start to finish: 5 minutes prep + 45 minutes in the oven

May I be so bold as to suggest Sir and Madam might fancy this on a Friday night? Perfect with a bottle of wine, an episode of your favourite DVD box set and a side order of end-of-week exhaustion. This meal takes minutes to prepare, but it still manages to feel special.

Pop the potatoes in a roasting tin and drizzle with oil; season with salt and pepper. Toss them so they are all well oiled. Put in the oven for 30 minutes, after which time the potatoes should be pretty much done.

Add the salmon to the tin, skin-side down. Add the halved artichokes, cut side down, and anchovies. Squeeze the lemon onto the salmon, add the wine and put the tin back in the oven for 15 minutes.

Remove from the oven and with a fork, flake the salmon to check it is cooked enough for you – pink in the middle is nice.

Serve (don't forget to scrape up the crunchy bits of anchovy!) and scatter with parsley.

Claire

Artichoke hearts I have to say these weren't often on my shopping list, due to their expense. They may be delicious, last for ages in the oil, and be a yummy addition to any of the mezze-style meals I often cobble together, but I couldn't quite stump up the cash. And then I discovered artichoke hearts in a tin. Half the price, obviously different, but still delicious. I now buy them all the time. I stick them into dishes like the above and whizz any leftover artichokes into pâté with cream cheese and a couple of anchovy fillets.

VERY SIMPLE *beef stew*

4 onions
3 tbsp vegetable oil
4 slices of bacon, chopped
800g (1¾ lb) shin of beef/shank, cut
   into chunks
350g (12 oz) carrots (use little
   carrots whole, or chunk normal-
   sized carrots)
3 tbsp flour
100ml (scant ½ cup) red wine
500ml (2¼ cups) beef stock/bouillon
1 level tbsp tomato purée/paste
sprig of thyme
2 bay leaves
1 French loaf
Dijon mustard
salt and pepper

Start to finish: 30 minutes prep
+ 2½ hours cooking

Serves: 4

Claire's confession I never peel carrots. There. I've said it. Are you still reading? What do you think of me and my slatternly ways? I'd like to say it's because I want to reduce waste and I've heard there are more nutrients in the skin than elsewhere in a carrot. But really? I'm just lazy. But you knew that already.

My argument is that carrot peel is so thin and tasteless, it doesn't bother me if it is there or not. In which case, why spend extra time in the kitchen peeling?

Oh, I do love beef. I cook it so rarely, but when I do, I like to make a fuss of it. This dish is made with shin of beef/shank, more commonly known as stewing steak – the cheapest beef cut. But to those in the know, it's also the most flavoursome. It needs a little TLC, at least two hours in the oven, but then you're rewarded with a melt-in-the mouth experience.

Preheat the oven to 180°C/350°F/gas mark 4.

Peel the onions and cut each of them into eighths.

Heat the vegetable oil in a medium-sized cast iron casserole dish with a lid. Once hot, add the bacon and fry until browned. Remove with a slotted spoon and add the chunks of beef and cook until browned on all sides. You may need to do this in a few batches. Remove with a slotted spoon.

Reduce the heat and put the onions and carrots in the dish. Fry until the vegetables are slightly coloured and then remove with a slotted spoon.

Now the dish just contains the oil left by the meat and vegetables. Stir in the flour until it is well mixed in – this is the beginning of a roux and should turn light brown. Add the wine, stock, tomato purée/paste and thyme. Stir until it is a smooth mixture and bring to the boil, still stirring. If it doesn't turn into a smooth mixture, and you have lumps of flour which refuse to disappear, don't worry – they will after 2½ hours in the oven.

Pop the meat and vegetables back into the dish with all their juices, season with salt and pepper and add the bay leaves. Put the lid on the casserole dish, and put the whole lot in the oven for 2 hours – give it a stir halfway through.

Cut the French loaf into eight slices. Spread Dijon mustard on one side of each slice. After the casserole has been cooking for 2 hours, put the bread into the stew, pushing it down into the juices. Alternate between placing the mustard face up and face down. Pop the whole lot back in the oven, uncovered, for 30 minutes. Serve with a salad, if you feel the need, or some cabbage wilted in butter and lemon juice.

CHICKEN, CHORIZO
and lentils

a splash of olive oil
1 large chicken – the bigger it is,
    the more leftovers
100g (3½ oz) chorizo
2 leeks, finely chopped
2 garlic cloves, chopped
2 celery sticks, chopped
1 carrot, finely chopped
300g (1½ cups) green lentils
3 tbsp white wine
about 500ml (2 cups) chicken
    stock/bouillon
3 sprigs of thyme
10 cherry tomatoes
salt and plenty of pepper

Start to finish: 30 minutes prep
and cooking + 90 minutes in
the oven

Serves: 4–6

Hearty, wholesome and perfect for a weekend lunch or dinner. There's a bit of chopping and frying at the beginning, but once it's in the oven pour yourself a nice glass of wine and relax – 90 minutes later lunch is ready. Make it with as big a bird as you can and pop the leftovers in the freezer. Alternatively, follow the cheats below and make it super-fast for a mid-week, post-work supper.

Preheat the oven to 180°C/350°F/gas mark 4.

Get your biggest flameproof casserole dish with a lid and put it on the hob/stovetop. Throw in a couple of glugs of oil, enough to cover the base of the dish once it's heated.

Rub salt and pepper into the chicken and then fry the whole bird in the casserole dish, until golden on all sides.

Transfer the chicken to a plate and put the chorizo, leeks, garlic, celery and carrot in the casserole. Fry on a gentle heat until their colour begins to change. Then throw in the lentils – give them a good stir, coating them in the oil. Splosh in a little white wine, turn up the heat and let it sizzle and evaporate – this means you keep the flavour but lose most of the alcohol. Stir everything a bit and then add the chicken stock, enough to thoroughly cover the lentils and vegetables. Add the thyme, the tomatoes and pop the chicken on top of the lentils. Cover the dish with the lid and put in the oven for 90 minutes.

When the time is up, pull a leg away from the body – it should come away easily if it is properly cooked, otherwise it will need a bit longer. Put the chicken on a plate and shred the meat. Check the seasoning of the lentils. Use a ladle to put the lentils and vegetable broth in a wide dish. Place the shredded chicken over the top.

Super-fast cheats If you want this as a quick after-work supper, you can do exactly the same thing, but use vacuum-packed cooked lentils (they are double the weight of raw lentils), so if you are making this for 4–6 people, you need about 600g (21 oz) of cooked lentils and chicken thighs/drumsticks. Then the whole dish needs only about 15–20 minutes in the oven, rather than 90.

CHERRY TOMATO TART
with mozzarella and basil

INGREDIENTS

1 x 320g puff pastry sheet
(17 oz sheet)
2 tbsp pesto
125g (4 oz) mozzarella cheese
8 cherry tomatoes, sliced
a splash of milk, to glaze
some basil leaves

Start to finish: 5 minutes prep
+ 12–15 minutes in the oven

Serves: 4

Dinner need never be more than 20 minutes away if you have a packet of puff pastry to hand. Just combine with three or more random ingredients from the fridge and a scrumptious supper is yours after just a few minutes in the oven. Here's how.

Remove the pastry from the fridge 10 minutes before you are going to use it. This stops it cracking as you unfurl it. Preheat the oven to 220°C/425°F/gas mark 7.

Lightly flour or line a large baking sheet, then unroll the pastry onto it. Using a blunt knife, draw a line 1.5cm (⅛ inch) from the edges of the pastry. This will be your border.

With a fork, prick inside the pastry border lots of times – this should stop the inside of the tart from puffing up too much. Then paint with pesto using a pastry brush or the round end of a spoon.

Rip the mozzarella into thin strips and place evenly over the top of the pesto. Dot the slices of cherry tomato over the cheese.

Using the blunt knife again, lightly score the borders with a criss-cross pattern and then paint them with milk so they go a deeper brown when they are baked.

Pop in the oven and bake for 12–15 minutes, until the border puffs up. Remove and scatter with basil leaves.

A slapdash guide to puff pastry
The above is less a recipe and more an idea. A starting-off point. If you don't have mozzarella in the fridge, why not try Cheddar? Stilton? Goat's cheese? Just about anything, to be honest. You only need a combination of the following:

Pastry Shop-bought puff pastry sheets – obviously. Don't bother with the roll-your-own blocks. Once you've cleared a space on your counter, cleaned it, found the rolling pin, floured everything, rolled the pastry and cleared up, you may as well have made the pastry in the first place.

A base Pesto, tomato purée/paste, onion marmalade.

A topping Mushrooms, tomatoes, broccoli, smoked salmon, asparagus. Use whatever you have in the fridge that will cook properly in around 15 minutes. If you're not sure it will cook in that time, just pre-cook and then put it on. For example, slow-fry leeks in olive oil until they are translucent, stir in some double/heavy cream, thyme, season and then plonk on the pastry and bake.

Cheese Whatever you've got. Really.

Some suggestions
Onion marmalade, goat's cheese and figs
Ham, olive tapenade and feta cheese
Asparagus, Parma ham and mozzarella over pesto

lucy

OVEN-BAKED
bolognese

I was brought up on minced/ground beef and while others scorn, I love its versatility. You can do so much with it! This version can be eaten in a lasagne, with pasta or rice, or just by changing a few ingredients, in a cottage pie or a chilli. I got the idea of oven baking it from a Delia Smith recipe. She uses minced pork and beef and adds chicken livers to the meat, which is delicious, but a bit over-the-top for this mid-week staple.

Traditionally, you should use *soffrito* (chopped onions, carrots and celery) but my children spend the whole meal picking out the 'bits' so I have admitted defeat and just use chopped onions.

Preheat the oven to 160°C/325°F/gas mark 3.

In a large saucepan (or a flameproof casserole dish with a lid) heat the oil and fry the onions until soft. Add the beef and cook until it has browned. Using your wooden spoon – or even better, a wooden fork – make sure all the strands of meat are separated. There is nothing guaranteed to remind you more of school dinners than chunks of mince.

Take off the heat and add the tomatoes, tomato purée/paste, bay leaves and rosemary. Season with salt and pepper. Give it a good stir. Put the lid on and put it into the oven for 3 hours. Ignore it completely. When you come back, it will have been transformed into the most delicious, soft, tasty bolognese imaginable.

I make this in bulk and freeze half (if you don't want to do this, just halve the quantities as this makes a lot!). Serve stirred through spaghetti, with grated Parmesan cheese on top.

INGREDIENTS

olive oil
2 onions, chopped
1kg (2¼ lb) minced/ground beef
3 x 400g (14 oz) tins of tomatoes
200g (¾ cup) tomato purée/paste
2 bay leaves
1 sprig of rosemary
salt and pepper

Start to finish: 10 minutes prep + 3 hours in the oven

Serves: 8

Marvellous mince! Use beef stock/bouillon instead of tomatoes for a cottage pie filling. Or omit the bay leaves and rosemary and add 1 tsp chilli powder (or to taste) for a chilli, adding a tin of rinsed kidney beans near the end of cooking.

MR PLOWMAN'S
fish stew

INGREDIENTS

1kg (2¼ lb) mussels
1 tbsp olive oil
1 large onion, chopped
3 garlic cloves, chopped
100g (3½ oz) chorizo, sliced
500g (18 oz) white fish fillets
    skin on, chopped into chunks,
1 tbsp smoked paprika
100ml (scant ½ cup) white wine
600ml (2½ cups) fish stock/bouillon
500g (18 oz) prawns/shrimp
bunch of fresh coriander/cilantro,
    thyme or flat-leaf parsley,
    chopped
salt and pepper
crusty bread, to serve

Start to finish: 10 minutes prep
+ 20 minutes cooking

Serves: 4

Who is Mr Plowman? And why would we want his fish stew? Trust us. We can vouch for both. Mr Plowman is Claire's husband and his fish stew is delectable. This is a lovely Friday or Saturday night supper, good enough to serve to friends. Regard the ingredients list as a kind of pick and mix. Leave out what you don't like, add more of what you do – the mussels could become a mussel-and-clam combo, the prawns (big or small) can be shell on or off, the fish could be coley, haddock or pollock …

Wash and beard the mussels (this means pulling out the little weedy bits in the shell). Give any open ones a tap and discard if they don't close.

Heat the oil in a large pot with a lid and gently fry the onion for 2–3 minutes, then add the garlic and cook for a further minute. Add the sliced chorizo and cook until well browned on both sides, which takes about 4 minutes.

Add the white fish skin-side down, and fry for 4 minutes, turning halfway through. Add the paprika and stir well. Season with salt and pepper. Add the wine and fish stock and bring to the boil.

Add the mussels to the pot, bring back to the boil, put the lid on and boil for 7–8 minutes until all the mussels are open. Discard any that aren't. Add the prawns/shrimp during the last minute of cooking. Add the coriander/cilantro, thyme or parsley, stir and check seasoning.

Serve in bowls with crusty bread.

crowd pleasers

Smile! Your guests are here! So what if the chicken is still pink and those potatoes won't crisp up? Just don't let anyone see you cry. Cooking for a crowd can fray the hardiest of nerves. The pressure of appearing in control in the kitchen, while ensuring your children don't kill each other and making polite conversation about the state of the nation is hard work.

But cooking for a crowd needn't be something to fear. Honest. The key is to keep it simple and make dishes where all the hard work is done before you open the front door – grin intact.

Our Emergency Roast Chicken (see page 110), cooked in just 40 minutes, and Roast Rib of Beef (see opposite) will revolutionise those relaxed (ha!) weekend meals when you invite your friends over. None of our recipe suggestions involve gravy – far too much last-minute stress. Instead let us introduce you to Muhammara (see page 111) and Salsa Verde (see page 108). If you've not yet made either, get ye to the kitchen pronto. Both can be made in advance and snazz up almost anything.

One tip (we know it sounds obvious, but bear with us) is to start cooking in plenty of time. Covered in foil, meat can rest for ages and lots of our dishes (Potato Dauphinoise for example, see page 104) won't mind being kept warm in a low oven for a while. Follow the advice in this chapter and you will be able to make lunch for the PTA without breaking into a sweat, or a bottle of gin. Let us know how it goes.

3-rib piece of beef (approx. 2.5kg/5½ lb)
2 tsp plain/all-purpose flour
2 tsp English mustard powder
salt and pepper

Start to finish: 10 minutes prep + 1 hour cooking

Serves: 8

The only panic-inducing thing about this recipe is the price. This is a very expensive cut of meat, but my goodness it is worth it! It is for when the boss or prospective parents-in-law are coming to visit (just make sure they are not vegetarian – it has cow ribs poking out of it). The one thing that won't induce panic is the cooking method. Hot and fast, the whole piece of meat takes under 1 hour. Delicious with Pea Stew and Potato Dauphinoise (see overleaf).

Take the beef out of the fridge half an hour before cooking to bring it to room temperature.

Preheat the oven to 240°C/475°F/ gas mark 9.

Rub the meat all over with the flour and mustard powder. Season with salt and pepper.

Put the meat in a sturdy roasting dish – fat side up – and then put it in the oven for 50 minutes. The layer of fat across the top of the beef is what keeps it moist and succulent. It dries up a bit like crackling and is delicious to eat. Baste it occasionally with the beautiful beef dripping that will ooze out of it.

It may seem crazy to roast meat at such a high temperature, but as it is for such a short time, it doesn't overcook and turns out unbelievably succulent. It is probably my favourite recipe in this entire book.

After 50 minutes, reduce the temperature to 190°C/375°F/gas mark 5 for 5 minutes. The beef should be charred slightly on the outside, but will be beautifully pink in the middle. Of course leave it for longer if you like your meat well done.

Remove from the oven. Double-wrap with aluminium foil and leave to rest for up to 30 minutes. There should be a collective sigh of pleasure as the meat is carved, and quite right too!

Lucy

leftovers If there is any left over, it is great in a stir-fry or in a sandwich with horseradish and watercress. The cooked meat freezes well (but freeze it in one piece to prevent it from drying out). Once defrosted, if you chop it up small, it can be turned into a delicious cottage pie.

16 spring onions/scallions,
    finely sliced
170g (10 tbsp) unsalted butter
    (eek!)
4 heads Little Gem lettuce,
    shredded
600g (1 lb 4 oz) frozen petits pois
300ml (1⅓ cups) hot chicken
    stock/bouillon
salt and pepper

Start to finish: 5 minutes prep
+ 30 minutes cooking

Serves: 8 as a side

1.2kg (2¾ lb) Maris Piper or
    King Edwards potatoes
    (or Yukon Gold or Russet)
2 garlic cloves
600ml (2½ cups) double/heavy
    cream
salt and pepper

Start to finish: 20 minutes prep
+ 90 minutes in the oven

Serves: 8 as a side

A less rich version Substitute chicken stock/bouillon for the cream and layer the potatoes with thinly sliced onions (ending on a potato layer) adding the odd bay leaf. Then pour over enough stock to cover the potatoes and bake. This is called pommes boulangère.

PEA stew

Oh to be French! To eat cheese for breakfast and make love before lunch. They are a nation of poets, philosophers and gourmands and we have them to thank for this (and many other) dishes. In English, this would probably be called pea stew, but in France it is known as *Petits Pois à la Française*.

Fry the spring onions/scallions in the butter until soft. Stir in the lettuce and when it is wilted, add the frozen peas. Stir for a bit; the peas will look a bit forlorn and clumpy but this is normal. Add the stock. Stir until the peas defrost. It will be looking a bit better now!

Simmer for about 20 minutes, uncovered, until the buttery liquid is reduced and you are left with a tender pan of perfect peas. Season with salt and pepper. Voila!

POTATO dauphinoise

This is the humble potato's sex bomb moment. The glasses come off, the hair comes down! *Bonjour, Madamoiselle Pomme de Terre.* Slow-cooking potatoes with garlic and cream turns a prosaic favourite into a scene-stealer. Yum.

Preheat the oven to 160°C/325°F/gas mark 3. Peel the garlic cloves and rub them all over the sides and bottom of a large gratin dish.

Peel the potatoes, then either using a mandolin or a very sharp knife (or the slicing attachment on a food processor) slice the potatoes. They should be about 3mm (⅛ inch) thick. As you slice, place the potatoes into a mixing bowl. When they are all sliced, pour over the cream and add the salt and pepper. Gently mix them so everything is nicely covered.

Pour them into the gratin dish and push them down, so there are no gaps and it feels quite solid. The cream should not quite cover the top layer of potato, but just be peeking through from underneath. Bake for 90 minutes. After 45 minutes check they're not browning too quickly (place foil over them if they are). If the cream looks like it is separating, turn the oven down.

The key to these is to cook them slowly. They can be started before your guests arrive and then kept warm in a low oven. They always take longer to cook than you think and there is nothing worse than the taste of undercooked potatoes. So to make sure yours have their ooh la la! moment, leave plenty of time.

ROSEMARY AND ANCHOVY
leg of lamb with lentils & salsa verde

1 leg of lamb (approx 2.3kg/5 lb)
6 garlic cloves, crushed
25g (1 oz) anchovies
4 sprigs of rosemary, finely chopped
2 tbsp olive oil
150ml (⅔ cup) water, red wine or combination of both
salt and pepper

Start to finish: Hmm, tricky to estimate and depends whether you have a food processor. If not, 60 minutes of prep dotted throughout the day + cooking time (see below)

Serves: 6 (plus leftovers)

Imagine the scene: the doorbell goes. You answer it. Rather than the usual white knuckles around a wooden spoon and a rictus grin, you greet your friends and their children with a relaxed smile. Then the smell of roasting lamb wafts towards them. Oh the joy! This can be more than just a fantasy. Roast lamb can be prepared hours in advance, as can the salsa and lentils (see overleaf), leaving you with oodles of time to practise those open door/smile moves.

Take the lamb out of the fridge half an hour before putting it in the oven to bring it to room temperature, which helps it cook more evenly.

Preheat the oven to 230°C/450°F/gas mark 8. Put an oven rack in the lower half of the oven, leaving space above it for the leg of lamb to sit.

Make the marinade by crushing the garlic and anchovies together in a pestle and mortar. Add the finely chopped rosemary leaves. Mix together.

Cut 2-cm/¾-inch deep slits a couple of centimetres apart (about 1 inch), all over the lamb. Rub olive oil all over the lamb. Then scoop up the marinade and press it into the slits as well as rubbing it all over the leg. Generously season with salt and pepper.

Place 150ml (⅔ cup) water, red wine or a bit of both in a roasting tin, add the lamb and put it in the oven. Cook according to the timings in the box below. Once cooked, remove from the oven and let the lamb rest, covered with foil and a folded tea towel, for at least 20 minutes.

Cooking lamb by numbers
There's nothing more annoying than following a recipe and then realising that your joint of meat is a different size to the one in the recipe, and not being quite sure what your cooking times should be. So, to make your life a little easier…

Under 2kg/4½ lb
20 minutes in a very hot oven (230°C/450°F/gas mark 8), then turn it down to 160°C/325°F/gas mark 3). Cook it for 10 minutes per 500g/lb for rare, 15 minutes per 500g/lb for medium, and 20 minutes per 500g/lb for well done.

Over 2kg/4½ lb
30 minutes in a very hot oven (230°C/450°F/gas mark 8), then turn it down to 160°C/325°F/gas mark 3). Cook it for 10 minutes per 500g/lb for rare, 15 minutes per 500g/lb for medium, and 20 minutes per 500g/lb for well done.

Note
Allow about 300g/10½ oz meat per adult when buying a bone-in joint of meat. Then add a bit more for leftovers.

LENTILS

1 onion, chopped
1 tbsp olive oil
2 garlic cloves, chopped
600g (3½ cups) lentils
200ml (scant 1 cup) chicken
    stock/bouillon
large knob of butter
bunch of mint, chopped

Start to finish: 5 minutes prep
+ 30 minutes cooking

Serves: 6

Claire

Serve the lentils, topped with a few hearty slices of lamb per plate and salsa verde drizzled all over.

Fry the onion in the olive oil until soft, then add the garlic and fry for another minute.

Add the lentils and gently fry for 1 minute. Don't add any salt at this early stage or your lentils will take forever to cook. Add enough water to cover the lentils and bring to the boil. Turn the heat down to a very gentle simmer, topping the water up when it starts to boil dry. After about 15–20 minutes, the lentils should have a nice consistency – soft enough to eat, but with a bit of bite. Add the stock/bouillon, and give them another 5–10 minutes.

Remove from the heat and cover. When you are ready to serve, check that your lentils are moist, but without too much excess liquid – if there's too much, drain, then add a large knob of butter, and stir in the mint.

SALSA *verde*

INGREDIENTS

½ bunch of flat-leaf parsley,
    chopped
½ bunch of basil, chopped
2 tbsp capers, chopped
½ x 50g (2 oz) tin of anchovies
2 garlic cloves, crushed
juice of ½ lemon
1 tbsp red wine vinegar
1 tsp Dijon mustard
6 tbsp olive oil
salt and pepper

Start to finish: 10 minutes

Serves: 6

This is an easy thing to make while the lentils are cooking. You can keep an eye on them, making sure they don't boil dry while you get busy chopping.

Using a food processor (in an ideal world) or a sharp knife, chop the herbs. Chop the capers and anchovies, again either by hand or in a food processor. Crush the garlic in a pestle and mortar or garlic crusher. Then mix them all together in a bowl, along with the lemon, vinegar and mustard. Add the olive oil gradually until you have a thick, but pourable sauce. Add salt and pepper to taste.

Cover and put it in the fridge. It will keep for a day or so.

AUBERGINE PARMESAN
with a hazelnut crust

INGREDIENTS

2 aubergines/eggplants
olive oil
salt
75g (¾ cup) Parmesan cheese,
    grated
200g (1½ cups) mozzarella
    cheese, shredded

Tomato sauce
Double quantities of Everyday
    Italian Tomato Sauce
    (see page 39)

Hazelnut crust
60g (½ cup) hazelnuts
4 handfuls of breadcrumbs
1 tbsp grated Parmesan cheese
2 tbsp olive oil

Start to finish: 30 minutes prep
+ 25 minutes in the oven

Serves: 4–6

Despite some of our best friends being vegetarian, entertaining them can be tricky. Nothing personal and it's not that we don't love vegetables, but it can be hard to find a veggie dish that feels sufficiently special for a dinner party. Enter Aubergine Parmesan with a Hazelnut Crust. This is special. Hearty layers of aubergine/eggplant, set among mozzarella cheese, tomato sauce and Parmesan cheese, are topped with a crunchy, nutty crumb. It can be made in advance and popped in the oven just before your guests are due.

Preheat the oven to 220°C/425°F/gas mark 7.

Make the tomato sauce (see page 39).

Line two baking sheets with baking paper. Slice the aubergine/ eggplant into 1-cm (⅜-inch) thick slices. Make sure they are not any thicker, or they may be a little unwieldy and spongy. Lay them on the sheets, brush their tops with olive oil and sprinkle with salt. Put in the oven for about 7 minutes – until they are browned. Then turn them over and do the same to the other side.

While they are cooking, make the hazelnut crust. Toast the hazelnuts in a frying pan for a minute or two, shaking them around and then place in a clean tea/dish towel. Rub them hard and their brown skins should come off in the towel. You don't need to be scrupulous, just get most of the skins off.

Then crush the nuts – put them in a freezer bag and bang it with a rolling pin for some stress release. Again, the nuts don't need to be uniformly pulverised, just bashed about a bit – some big pieces, some small. Put them in a bowl and add the breadcrumbs, cheese and oil. Mix.

Once the aubergines are out of the oven, turn the temperature down to 200°C/400°F/gas mark 6, if you are going to be cooking the dish immediately. If you are not cooking it until later, turn the oven off.

Oil the sides and base of an ovenproof dish – I use a 25 x 32cm (10 x 13 inch) ceramic one. Pour a thin layer of sauce over the base. Cover the sauce with a layer of roasted aubergine. Spoon some sauce over that layer and then put about half the shredded mozzarella and half the Parmesan over that. Add another layer of aubergine, another layer of sauce and then both the remaining cheeses. Scatter the hazelnut crumbs on top.

Put in the oven for 20–25 minutes, until the top is brown and bubbling. Let it cool a little before serving.

EMERGENCY *roast chicken*

INGREDIENTS

1.1kg (2½ lb) whole chicken
butter
1 lemon
salt and pepper

Start to finish: 2 minutes prep
+ 40 minutes cooking +
10 minutes resting

Serves: 4

Nobel Prize alert! Well not quite, but this emergency roast chicken recipe deserves some kind of award. It is stress-free cooking at its best. In just 40 minutes a whole bird is roasted to succulent perfection. How? The key is a small bird (around 1.1kg/2½ lb) and a hot oven. Serve with Flatbreads and Muhammara – see opposite. If you want some greens, the Greek-Style Green Beans with Tomato (see page 53) are excellent with this dish.

Preheat the oven to 220°C/425°F/gas mark 7.

Smear the chicken with butter, not neglecting its wings and legs. Season generously with salt and pepper. Place the chicken in a roasting tin. Cut the lemon in half. Put one half inside the chicken and the other underneath it.

Roast in the oven for 40 minutes. Allow it to rest for 10 minutes before carving.

FLATBREADS

INGREDIENTS

250g (scant 2 cups) plain/all-
   purpose flour
1 tsp salt
1 tbsp olive oil
150ml (⅔ cup) warm water

Start to finish: 5 minutes prep
+ 15 minutes cooking

Makes: 8

These flatbreads are very easy to prepare and can be made in the time it takes to walk to the shops and buy some. They can either be prepared in advance or served straight from the pan.

Put the flour and salt into a large mixing bowl. Combine the oil and warm water in a jug, and then pour it into the flour mixture with one hand while mixing the ingredients together with the other. This is called multi-tasking.

Once you've got a dough (add a splash more water if it is too floury or sprinkle with some more flour if too wet), place it on a floured worktop and knead for 5 minutes. Or, if you have a food mixer, let a dough hook work its magic. Put it into a bowl, cover with a damp tea towel and set aside for 15 minutes to allow it to rise a little.

Using a knife, divide the dough into 8 pieces and with a rolling pin roll each portion into a circle about the size of a side plate.

Cook in a dry frying pan, over a medium heat for about a minute on each side or until lightly browned and slightly bubbly.

Serve straight away or stack on a plate and keep warm in a low oven.

lucy

MUHAMMARA

This spicy walnut and red pepper dip from the Middle East is an unusual, but delightful, accompaniment to roast chicken. It is loaded with vegetables and is great smeared on the flatbread or just eaten alongside the chicken.

INGREDIENTS

100g (¾ cup) walnuts
3 roasted red peppers (I always buy
   mine ready roasted in a jar)
100g (2 cups) fresh breadcrumbs
1 small red chilli, deseeded
1 small onion, finely chopped
2 garlic cloves, crushed
1 tbsp pomegranate molasses
1 tbsp lemon juice
1 tsp ground cumin
2 tbsp extra virgin olive oil
salt and pepper

Start to finish: less than 10 minutes

Serves: enough for 4, with leftovers

Toast the walnuts in a dry frying pan until they are lightly browned. It should only take 5 minutes, but be careful not to let them catch.

Next, put them in a food processor (or a bowl if you are using a hand-held mixer) along with the remaining ingredients. Whizz until smooth. Pour in the olive oil. Whizz some more. That's it.

box fresh

There are few weekday mornings when we don't leap enthusiastically out of bed, propelled mainly by our joy at having to knock up a couple of packed lunches. Crisps? Yes! Sandwiches? Yes! (At this point we usually punch the air.) Fruit easily eaten with little hands? Yes, yes, yes!!!

Packed lunchboxes – we all love 'em. The strange stale smell they emit at the end of the day. The random fruit leftovers we find months later, hidden in small people's bedrooms. The way they challenge our sanity first thing in the morning. But if your kids refuse to eat school dinners, they are part of your life and (deep breath) we just have to get on with it.

To help make life a little easier we've come up with a selection of make-ahead recipes, so there's no crazed rush before school. Just the popping of Parmesan and Spinach Muffins (see page 118) into a paper bag, a smug scooping of Potato Salad Plus (see page 121) into a container, the relaxed wrapping of Sausage Rolls with Onion Marmalade (see page 119) in foil. Our other suggestions (we hesitate to call them recipes) are more an arrangement of foods. Little bags of Nuts, Berries and Chocolate Chips (see page 117) always go down a treat, and as you are making (ok, ok, arranging) them, you can ensure that the chocolate/fruit/nut ratio is one you agree with.

In the same vein are our suggestions for the sandwich section. Whenever we ask the experts (a.k.a. fellow parents who respond to our blog) what their top secrets are for packed lunches, they say kids love a bit of DIY. So self-assembly (such as getting the kids to do the hard work of putting together the wraps/dipping the dips etc.) is the name of the game. Read on for more shortcuts . . .

LUNCHBOXES

If there is one piece of parenting advice we can impart, it is – no matter how much they protest – make your children have school dinners. Packing a lunch, half-dressed, piece of toast hanging from your mouth, while trying to herd cats, sorry children, is not conducive to family life. No matter how organised you try to be, there will be some mornings when your children go to school with some chocolate cake and a packet of cheese puffs rattling around their lunchbox. Yes, you have become one of the parents you read about in the tabloids. If packed lunches are unavoidable, here are ten tips to make it easier on yourself.

Prepare as much as you can the night before. One of the rules of parenthood is that everything takes 20 times longer in the morning.

Sandwiches need to be made the morning they are eaten, otherwise they won't be very fresh (see our sandwich making guide on page 130). If that sounds like hell, then give them something they can assemble themselves…a wrap, some grated cheese and cucumber sticks, for example. Or you could butter bread the night before and get the fillings ready to assemble in the morning.

Variety is the spice of life You don't want cheese and pickle sandwiches five times a week, neither does your child.

Fruit There seems to be a relationship between fruit size and the speed at which it is eaten. Small children like fruit chopped up small. We know. Lazy! Spritz it with lemon juice, so it doesn't go brown. Dried fruit (see our Nuts, Berries and Chocolate Chips on page 117) is always popular.

A lunchbox isn't a lunchbox without *crisps*. Baked versions can be healthier than their fried cousins, or try mini breadsticks.

Dips Hummus, cream cheese, tzatziki (see page 120) are your friends. Pack them with crackers and crudités.

If dips are your friend, then *Tupperware* is your ideal husband. Tough, dependable and with a lifetime guarantee. Just owning it is a fast track to being (well, feeling?!) organised. It protects fruit from getting squashed, means you can buy biscuits and cookies in bulk and dispense appropriately, and serve up last night's leftovers for the next day's lunch with smug ease.

You have to give them *something sweet*, even if you don't want to. Bulk baking something like breakfast bars (see page 14) is a compromise, that will save you both time and money. Add chocolate chips if you want them to be eaten. If they have a savoury tooth, give them a chunk of cheese instead.

Check the labels of so-called healthy *fruit drinks*. Many of them aren't healthy or even particularly fruity. 100% fruit juice is best (To minimise the risk of tooth decay, fruit juice is best drunk with food). But what's wrong with water? Buy them a groovy reusable water bottle as an incentive. Add a squeeze of fresh lemon or lime juice if they complain the flavour is boring.

As a treat, albeit it slightly more labour intensive, breaded chicken dippers with noodles and sweetcorn can easily be made the night before and are perfect for family days out or school trips.

Peer pressure When they are young, children may be happy to munch on boiled eggs, but they will come to an age when they don't want their lunchboxes to stand out from their friends. Rejecting what your parents want you to eat is a normal part of growing up. So a lunchbox isn't a time to challenge their taste buds. You want to be sure they eat properly, so listen to them and work out which foods you are both happy with.

SPEEDY GONZALES *noodles*

INGREDIENTS

garlic-infused oil
handful of cooked frozen prawns/
   shrimp
handful of frozen peas
300g (10 oz) ready-cooked
   noodles
1 egg, beaten
soy sauce

Start to finish: about 4 minutes

Serves: 2 children

If you haven't discovered ready-cooked noodles in your local supermarket, then that epiphany is alone worth the price of this book. We promise. They are part-cooked (more tasty than it sounds) which means they can be fried in a pan in 90 seconds. So you can have a meal on the table for your offspring in less time than it takes to make a cup of tea. Make double and the next day's lunchbox is sorted too.

In a large frying pan heat some garlic-infused oil until it is properly hot. Add the frozen prawns and peas and cook for about 2 minutes, then add the noodles and cook for another 90 seconds, stirring all the time. Add the egg, still stirring, and a splash of soy sauce. This is very salty (which means kids love it!) so go easy for younger children. Decant into lunchboxes.

Serving suggestions

Replace the peas with sweetcorn/corn kernels, carrot ribbons or bean sprouts. You can also use meat left over from Sunday's roast, shredded and added to the pan with the peas. Just make sure that it is properly heated through.

Lucy

Freezer love The two foods I always have, without fail, in my freezer are peas and prawns/shrimp. They are the backbone to family food in my home because from them – and a few staples like stock/bouillon or pasta – a meal can be conjured up even when the rest of the fridge is depressingly desolate.

Let's take peas. They can be eaten as a side dish, go into rice, noodles or pasta, be whizzed up with stock to make soup, or dressed and served with feta cheese for a quick and easy salad (see page 87).

Prawns are often sold pre-cooked and can usually be cooked from frozen. They are packed full of protein and relatively cheap. They are the perfect ingredient to jazz up a risotto, pasta or noodles, as well as making a great lunch when dressed with Marie Rose sauce (this is more or less mayonnaise mixed together with tomato ketchup, Tabasco sauce and a little lemon) or fried in garlic with chunks of chorizo (see page 123).

4 spring onions/scallions, finely
  chopped
100g (3½ oz) Cheddar cheese, grated
100g (3½ oz) thickly cut ham,
  chopped
1 tbsp pickle/relish
2 eggs, beaten
1 sheet shortcrust or puff pastry,
  cut into 4 circles (I trace around
  a saucepan lid 14cm/5½ inches
  wide)

Start to finish: 10 minutes prep
+ 25 minutes in the oven

Serves: 4

HAM, CHEESE
and pickle pasty

In the course of my marriage, my husband has introduced me to many things… Leonard Cohen, Kidderminster Harriers football club, strawberry daiquiris, but most of all, pasties. Other than the obligatory one on holiday in their native Cornwall, they were not part of my culinary vernacular. These days, well, a week wouldn't be a week without a pasty. Homemade ones are a completely different beast to those you find in service station shops, and if you are using ready-made pastry (which obviously you should) they take no time at all to rustle up. The pickle cuts through the richness of the cheese and the pastry quite beautifully. They travel well, so make the ideal companion for packed lunches and family days out.

Preheat the oven to 180°C/350°F/gas mark 4.

Mix together the spring onions, cheese, ham, pickle and half the beaten egg. Divide the mixture between the pastry circles, covering only half the surface with the filling.

Brush egg around the edges and then fold the pastry over and crimp the edges with your fingers, so each semicircle is tightly sealed. Transfer to a greased baking sheet.

Using a pastry brush, glaze with the remaining egg and bake for 20–25 minutes until golden.

lucy

Cracking combos Ham, cheese and pickle is just one suggestion. You can really play around with the ingredients although I would always suggest including cheese. My favourite combinations include ham, mozzarella and pesto, or Stilton, fried leeks and walnuts. If you have some leftover roast chicken, that would be lovely with some fried onion and chorizo. Likewise, if you have some leftover roast squash, it would be delicious with some feta cheese and sage.

NUTS, BERRIES
and chocolate chips

This is not strictly a recipe – more an assembly job, but sometimes eating well is not about cooking at all, just an idea and a clever shop. This healthy treat is perfect for packed lunches and long journeys. Although suitable for children, it is a winner with grown-ups too.

Simply take equal quantities of:

1 Your favourite unsalted nuts (boring though it may sound, peanuts work really well)

2 Dried fruit – different varieties of raisins, sour cherries and cranberries are delicious

3 Your favourite chocolate bashed up into little pieces (so, so much tastier than the cloying sweetness of shop-bought chocolate chips or chocolate buttons)

Pour all three ingredients into a freezer bag. Shake. Eat. The most effort you will expend is trying not to eat them before lunch. Of course, you can make this in bulk and store in a jar in the kitchen, but we cannot guarantee how long it will last...

FRIENDLY fruit kebabs

INGREDIENTS

4 strawberries
8 blueberries
4 red grapes
4 white grapes
4 small wooden kebab sticks

Start to finish: 2 minutes prep

Serves: 4

These are called friendly because for some reason children – especially smaller ones – can find eating whole pieces of fruit overwhelming. To them eating a banana can seem like climbing Everest. They are far more likely to eat fruit if it is cut up small or if you thread small pieces on to mini kebab sticks. As these have to travel, fruit that has skin works best – like red and white grapes and blueberries – plus strawberries. If eating straight away, add chunks of banana, kiwi and apple.

Thread the fruit on the kebab sticks. Squash-proof them by popping them in a Tupperware pot.

Top tip These kebabs are even friendlier if you alternate the fruit with an occasional marshmallow. Naughty but nice!

200g (7 oz) frozen spinach
    (it reduces to 100g/3½ oz after
    it's been cooked)
small knob of butter
250g (heaping 1¾ cups) plain/
    all-purpose flour
1 tbsp baking powder
½ tsp salt
75g (1 cup) grated Parmesan
    cheese
1 egg
240ml (1 cup) milk
90ml (6 tbsp) olive oil
salt and pepper

Start to finish: 10 minutes prep
+ 20 minutes in the oven

Makes: 10

PARMESAN
and spinach muffins

These savoury wonders will make your child's lunchbox the envy of their friends. Just split the muffin and smear with cream cheese and a slice of salami. Boom! The little monkeys will be begging for more. Just don't mention the spinach.

Preheat the oven to 190°C/375°F/gas mark 5. Put 10 paper muffin cases into a cupcake or muffin tin.

Cook the frozen spinach. Place it in a little water in a saucepan. Put it over the heat and cook until the frozen lump has dissolved. Transfer the spinach to a sieve and using a wooden spoon, squeeze out all the water. Stir in a little butter and some salt and pepper to give it some flavour and put to one side.

Put the flour, baking powder and salt into a mixing bowl. Stir in two thirds of the Parmesan and the spinach, until it is evenly distributed.

In a separate jug, measure out the egg, milk and olive oil. Give it a good stir to break up the egg and then pour into the dry ingredients. Stir, just enough to get rid of all pockets of dry flour, but you don't need to mix too much – unlike a cake batter it doesn't need air beaten into it.

Divide the mixture between the muffin cases, sprinkle the leftover Parmesan over the top and put in the oven. Bake for 20–25 minutes, until golden and a skewer comes out of the muffin clean.

Serve split and buttered, with a spot of cream cheese, some crunchy bacon or bit of salami.

Claire

Top tip If you don't have any muffin cases (or a muffin pan), just pop the batter into a buttered and lined loaf tin to make a Parmesan and Spinach Loaf. You may have to bake in the oven for a bit longer, so test by inserting a skewer or sharp knife into the loaf and see if it comes out clean. When done, cool on a wire rack and cut into slices. This works with any muffin recipe.

375g pack (¾ of a 17 oz package)
   all-butter ready-rolled puff pastry
   sheets
6 sausages
2 tbsp onion marmalade
1 egg, beaten

Start to finish: 10 minutes prep
+ 25 minutes baking

Makes: 6

SAUSAGE ROLLS
with onion marmalade

I live near a fabulous food shop – the *Grove Park Deli* – where they make the most delicious sausage and onion marmalade rolls. It is a clever twist on a well-loved British favourite and simple to make at home. The tartness of the marmalade provides a beautiful contrast to the savoury sausage.

Preheat the oven to 200°C/400°F/gas mark 6.

Take the pastry out of the fridge 10 minutes before you need to use it. It is much easier to work with if it is a little bit (but not too) warm.

Skin the sausages by running a sharp knife down their length and unpeeling them. This is actually quite fun.

Unroll the pastry and slice the sheet once lengthways down the middle and then horizontally into thirds. You should now have six equal portions of pastry. Brush some beaten egg on the long side of each piece. This is your 'glue' and will ensure your sausage roll doesn't unroll.

Put a sausage in the middle of each piece. Spread 1 tsp of marmalade on top of each. Roll the sausage in the pastry, pinching it together on the long side so it is firmly joined.

Lay the sausage rolls, join-side down, on a lined baking sheet. Brush the remaining egg over the top. Bake for 25 minutes until golden.

Lucy

TORTILLA CHIPS

INGREDIENTS

1 flour or corn tortilla wrap
olive oil
salt

Start to finish: 1 minute prep
+ 5 minutes cooking

Serves: 1

Ring the changes in your children's packed lunchbox (or yours for that matter) and give them these delicious homemade tortilla chips and dips. You could throw in some crudités for good measure. Simple, tasty and 100% moreish.

Preheat the oven to 180°C/350°F/gas mark 4.

Take a flour or corn tortilla wrap and brush it with olive oil on both sides. Sprinkle it with salt, then cut with scissors into eight triangles.

Spread all eight triangles onto a baking sheet and cook until lightly browned and crispy. Turn once during cooking. It should take about 5 minutes. Remove from the oven and cool.

TZATZIKI dip

INGREDIENTS

1 cucumber, peeled and deseeded
350g (1½ cups) Greek yogurt
2 garlic cloves, crushed
2 tbsp lemon juice
salt and pepper
olive oil

Start to finish: 5 minutes prep

Serves: 4

Grate the peeled and deseeded cucumber and remove any excess water by squeezing it either in your hand or popping it in a sieve and pressing down with a wooden spoon, until most of the water has gone.

Mix with the Greek yogurt in a bowl and stir in the crushed garlic and lemon juice. Sprinkle in some salt and pepper and finish with a drizzle of olive oil.

PESTO CREAM cheese dip

INGREDIENTS

1 tbsp green pesto (or to taste)
200g (7 oz) cream cheese
   (unbranded is half the price,
   and just as good!)

Start to finish: 1 minute prep

Serves: 4

Mix the pesto and cream cheese together in a small bowl. That's it! A yummy dip in seconds.

POTATO SALAD *plus*

575g (1¼ lb) baby new potatoes,
  cleaned
small bunch of parsley
3 spring onions/scallions
2 tsp capers
2 soft boiled eggs
2 tbsp mayonnaise
black pepper

Start to finish: 5 minutes prep +
20 minutes cooking

Serves: 4

This isn't any old potato salad. Full of wonderful savoury flavours, it is a delicious addition to your lunchbox. Make a batch on Sunday night and it will last until Wednesday. Each day you can pimp it up or dress it down. Serve alongside sandwiches, put it in a wrap with ham and mustard, or have it on its own with some added bacon and shredded chicken for a hearty homemade lunch.

Fill a large pan with cold water. halve the potatoes if they are bigger than bite size, then pop them in, bring to the boil and then simmer. Cook until they are tender.

While they are cooking, chop the parsley and the spring onions. Place in a medium-sized bowl. Add the capers. Peel the eggs and cut them into quarters.

Once the potatoes are cooked, cool them under cold running water, drain, cut into smaller pieces if necessary and add to the salad bowl. Stir in the mayonnaise, season with black pepper and stir well. Festoon with the soft boiled egg quarters.

CHAPTER 10

snacks & savoury morsels

We don't like to show favouritism, but if forced to choose a favourite chapter, then this would be it. Not that we don't LOVE all the other chapters (We do! We do! You're all gorgeous!), but when it comes to eating, these deliciously savoury morsels are what we could live on. Yes, we know it's not all about us, but we don't think we're alone.

These dishes are easy to love. They are all super-fast to prepare. Their ingredients are easy to get hold of – many are already in your cupboard – and they all pack a flavoursome punch. Baked Eggs with Smoked Mackerel en Cocotte (see page 124) takes almost as long to say as to prepare. Golden Carrot Fritters (see page 127) are a nice change and the ubiquity of the carrot means it's a rare day these can't be made. Bish Bash Bosh Burgers (see page 135) are as fast as they sound, but special enough for a Friday-night supper, as is Sizzling Chorizo and Prawns (see opposite).

This is low-effort, high-impact cooking, perfect for mid-week lunches when the thought of preparing yet another meal empties your brain. Great for a quick bite when the only thing in the fridge is a carrot, and just the ticket for a grown-up dinner in the evening when you want something tasty but quick.

SIZZLING CHORIZO
and prawns

INGREDIENTS

10-cm (4-inch) chunk of chorizo
a glug of olive oil
1 garlic clove
6 cooked and peeled king prawns/
    jumbo shrimp
1 tbsp dry sherry or white wine
salt and pepper

Start to finish: 10 minutes

Serves: 2 as an appetizer, or
serve double portions with bread
and salad as a main course

I first ate this on a hot London summer night in a friend's back garden. Fresh from the pan, it was served on a large platter with cocktail sticks (for spearing). All that was missing was sangria, and you could have been in Spain. The flavours and textures work perfectly together, but what I love most is its simplicity. Chorizo and prawns/shrimp are two of my store-cupboard staples and I sometimes make this as a greedy lunch for one, to be eaten with crusty bread to mop up the spicy juices.

Cut the chorizo (making sure you have peeled off the outer paper) into slices about the thickness of a pound coin (⅛ inch).

Heat the oil in a frying pan, toss in the chorizo and fry until it is crispy. The fat from the sausage mingles with the olive oil beautifully.

Crush the garlic clove into the pan, throw in the prawns/shrimp and cook until they are heated through. Add the tablespoon of sherry. Sizzle. Season. Serve.

Lucy

Frozen prawns If your prawns/shrimp are frozen, that's fine, just check the instructions as to whether they can be cooked from frozen – many can. If not, the best way to defrost is to leave them in the fridge overnight.

If you are reading this on Friday evening, with a frozen bag of prawns in your hand, don't despair. You can defrost them quickly by filling the kitchen sink with cold water, leaving the prawns in their plastic bag and popping them into the water. Keep the prawns in the plastic bag because if they directly touch the water, it will leach their flavour. After 30 minutes, change the water. You don't want the water to get too warm, as that will enable bacteria to develop. They should take less than an hour to defrost. If you can't wait an hour, open the bag, empty the prawns into a colander and place under cold running water. I won't tell anyone. Before you cook them, give them a squirt of lemon juice to revive their flavour.

BAKED EGGS
with smoked mackerel en cocotte

INGREDIENTS

butter, for greasing
1 smoked mackerel fillet
2 tbsp double/heavy cream
½ tsp Dijon mustard
pepper
2 eggs
chopped flat-leaf parsley, chives
    or dill (optional)

Start to finish: 5 minutes prep
+10 minutes in the oven

Serves: 2 children
or 1 adult

Doesn't everything sound better in French? *Petit chou* – cabbage. *Bouton* – spot or pimple. So it is that *en cocotte* or 'in a ramekin' gives baked eggs a certain glamour, a *je ne sais quoi*. It transforms a dish with just four ingredients into something more sophisticated. *Voila!* – a *petit pot* of deliciousness which is perfect for a quick lunch, brunch or hastily put together supper. *Bon appetit!*

Preheat the oven to 180°C/350°F/gas mark 4. Lightly butter two ramekin dishes and boil a kettle full of water.

Put a baking tray in the oven, ensuring there is enough room between the oven shelves for the baking tray which will soon contain the ramekins.

Flake the mackerel into a bowl with the cream and mustard. Season with pepper and stir.

Put the mackerel mix into the bottom of each buttered ramekin. Crack the eggs, carefully depositing each egg into each ramekin on top of the mackerel. Open the oven, place the ramekins in the oven tray, and pour boiling water into the tray so that it comes halfway up the ramekins.

Check after 10 minutes. The egg white should be set, but the yolk still runny. If you'd rather have your egg more cooked, put it back in the oven for a few more minutes. Once ready, scatter with chopped herbs and serve.

Serve with This is great without accompaniments for most kids. If your children are very young and you worry about giving them a hot ramekin, just scoop the contents out into a bowl. As a dinner for adults, this is delicious served alongside some wholemeal or sourdough toast, green salad and a glass of red wine.

Buy it! Smoked mackerel – delicious, distinctive and permanently in my fridge. Whizz it up with some crème fraîche and cream cheese for a superfast pâté lunch. Add a bit of horseradish for more depth. Or flake it into a salad. There's very little that isn't pepped up by a touch of smoked mackerel. Plus, it's cheap, lasts for ages in the fridge and is packed with omega-3s.

PINK *pancakes*

INGREDIENTS

2 eggs
250g (1¾ cups) plain/all-purpose
   or spelt flour
4 heaped tsp baking powder
couple of pinches of salt
200ml (scant 1 cup) milk
125g (1 cup) grated or puréed
   cooked beetroot/beets
1 tsp creamed horseradish
salt and pepper
vegetable oil
100g (scant ½ cup) cream cheese
small bunch of chives, chopped

Start to finish: 10 minutes to make
the batter + another 10–15 minutes
to cook

Serves: 4

It's not just little girls who are delighted by the novelty of these technicolor pancakes. Little boys wolf them down. Grown men ask for seconds. Easy to make, they are great for a weekend lunch. The beetroot/beet is incidental, the flavour isn't overpowering; it just lends the pancake a hint of earthiness. The horseradish gives some heat, but not enough to scare the children – up the quantities for a bit more of an adult kick.

Whisk the eggs in a large bowl with a fork until they are frothy. Add the flour, baking powder and salt. Pour in the milk and whisk until everything is combined. Stir in the beetroot/beets, horseradish and pepper.

Over a high heat, warm a large frying pan and drizzle on some vegetable oil.

Use a dessert spoon (or soup spoon) to drop the batter into the pan. You don't want the pancake to be any bigger as it will be too thick and won't cook through. Depending on the size of your pan, make two or three pancakes at a time.

Once you see bubbles come up to the centre of the pancake, flip it with a spatula and cook on the other side for a couple of minutes. Don't press it with a spatula, as that will reduce the amount of air inside, making your pancakes flat rather than fluffy.

Spread with the cream cheese, scatter with chives and season with pepper.

Serve with A dollop more of horseradish, flaked smoked mackerel fillets and chives make a sophisticated lunch. Make them mini-sized, and you've got a delicious canapé!

Got to love beetroot! Give beetroot/beets a chance if you're not already a convert. Cheap, nutritious and delicious. I always have vacuum-packed cooked beetroot in my fridge – it lasts for ages. If I need some pink colouring for cakes or icing, I just slit a hole in the packet (see note below), and some beetroot juice will come oozing out. A splash for pale pink and a bit more for a glorious dark red. The remaining beetroot can go into brownies or chocolate cake or whizz it up with the same amount of crème fraîche and a sprinkling of ground cumin for a delicious dip.

GOLDEN
carrot fritters

6 spring onions/scallions, finely
   chopped
4 carrots, about 500g (18 oz)
3 eggs
100g (¾ cup) plain/all-purpose flour
1½ tsp ground cumin
150g (5 oz) feta cheese
vegetable oil

To serve
flatbreads or flour tortillas
hummus
harissa (optional, and more
   for grown-ups)

Start to finish: 10 minutes prep
+ about 10 minutes frying

Serves: 4

Claire

You know those carrots in the fridge? The ones you're not quite sure what to do with? Fritter them. Turn them into a mass of golden deliciousness. Crispy, tasty balls of yum. It's so easy, takes minutes and surely that much carrot has got to be good for you? They are great for a quick lunch at home, as part of a more elaborate mezze-style dinner, or cold in a lunchbox with some hummus to dip.

Put the spring onions/scallions in a medium-sized bowl. Grate the carrots (no need to peel) into the same bowl. Add the eggs, flour and cumin and stir until well mixed. Crumble in the feta and stir. Season.

Heat the oil in a large saucepan. You want enough oil to cover the base of the saucepan. Once it is hot, use a dessertspoon to measure out the batter into the pan. Each spoonful is a fritter. Once the batter is in the oil, flatten it with the back of the spoon or with a spatula and leave the fritter for a minute or two until it has gone golden. Then, using a spatula, turn the fritter, flatten again, and wait until it goes golden. Remove from the pan.

While the fritters are cooking, heat up the tortillas by placing them directly on the hob's/stovetop's flames (if it's a gas hob). Just leave them there for a couple of seconds, otherwise they will burn, and then turn. Alternatively, dry-fry them in a frying pan. Place in a tea towel to keep warm, while you do the next one.

Spread hummus over the tortilla, and add a little harissa if you fancy. Then put a couple of the fritters in and wrap.

CHEESE & MARMITE
welsh rarebit

In our experience no child says no to cheese on toast. This delectable concoction has the same ingredients, and is just as easy. It is called Welsh Rarebit. Some Welsh Rarebits require a roux sauce, but this isn't one of them, meaning it's quicker. All to the good if you've got a baby on your hip, or hungry kids baying.

Preheat the grill/broiler to high. Toast the bread on both sides.

Mix the grated cheese with egg yolks, cream, Marmite and Worcestershire sauce. Add milk to get a nice consistency, so that the cheese mixture will be easy to spread on the toast.

Place the toast on some foil in a baking tray. Spoon on the cheese mixture and place under the grill. Cook for about 5 minutes and remove when it is brown and bubbling.

INGREDIENTS

2 slices of bread per person – crusty is nice, but whatever you have

200g (2 cups) grated hard cheese, usually Cheddar

2 egg yolks

1 tbsp cream

1 dessertspoon/soup spoon Marmite (yeast extract, see below)

a splash of Worcestershire sauce

1 tbsp milk

Start to finish: 5 minutes
+ 5 minutes under the grill/broiler

Serves: 2

love it or hate it? If you can't get hold of Marmite, or heaven forbid, don't like it, there are lots of alternatives. Bovril or Vegemite are the closest. However, you can also substitute a dash of mustard, some paprika, brown sauce, ketchup, whatever you have in the cupboard that you think your children will eat. Instead of the milk, you could use beer, but perhaps not if it's for children.

Claire

STRINGY TOMATO
pesto omelette

In the mad brain scramble that often follows the question: 'What shall we have for lunch?' I often overlook the simple pleasure of an omelette. Instead my brain whirrs and spews, I panic, and we end up with something convoluted and unnecessary, when all we needed was the delicious simplicity of eggs cooked in a pan. This version with mozzarella is a sure-fire hit.

Crack the eggs into a cup. Add a splash of water, some black pepper and a pinch of salt. Use a fork to break up the eggs and give them a bit of a stir.

Place a small non-stick frying pan (mine is 20cm/8 inch diameter) over a medium heat and add the butter. Once the butter has melted, add the chopped tomato. Fry until just slightly softened.

Once the pan is really hot, pour in the egg mixture and then, using a wooden spoon or spatula, bring in the outside edges of the omelette towards the middle slightly, so that the uncooked egg runs to the edge of the pan and cooks. After about 20 seconds, tilt the pan so the raw egg on top of the omelette is distributed evenly. After 30 seconds or so, the omelette should look more solid, but not cooked completely on top.

Tear the mozzarella up and lay it in the middle of the omelette. Spoon over the pesto and let the whole thing cook on a low heat for a little longer. Once cooked, the omelette should come easily away from the side of the pan when you pull it with a spatula.

Flip one side of the omelette over the other and slide onto your plate. Lunch is served.

INGREDIENTS

2 eggs
salt and pepper
knob of butter
1 small tomato, chopped
40g (1½ oz) mozzarella cheese
1 tsp pesto

Start to finish: 10 minutes

Serves: 1

MR O'BRIEN'S
top tips for tip-top sandwiches

Luckily for us, Lucy is married to the best sandwich maker in the western world, Mr O'Brien. A man who looks inside a fridge and doesn't see a piece of cheese, half a pot of pesto and a wilting lettuce, but potential.

Sandwiches must be the most versatile food in the world. Think how different a cucumber sandwich (white bread, no crusts, cucumber, salted butter) is to a chip butty (white roll, fish-shop chips/fries, salt, vinegar, ketchup, lettuce).

Just by changing the bread, the size, the fillings, crusts on/crusts off, you have a completely different dish.

We have the Earl of Sandwich to thank for this delicacy. He was an eighteenth-century aristocrat who ordered his valet to bring him meat tucked between two pieces of bread, and soon others began to order 'the same as Sandwich'! And thus the sandwich was created. Not many people can lay claim to inventing the world's most ubiquitous food and creating a new verb (sandwiched between …).

Upper-class men used to eat sandwiches while gambling at private clubs, but it wasn't until industrialisation that the masses got in on the act. Now we'd be lost without them.

Here are his tips...

Don't be shy Pile on the flavour. Unlike pizzas, more is more.

Experiment with spreads Try pesto, mayonnaise or mustard instead of butter. Whatever spread you are using, take it up to the edges of the bread. It acts as a barrier between bread and filling and will stop things going soggy.

To avoid onion breath, slice and chop, then soak your onions in cold water for 20 minutes.

Contrast is key Stick some capers or pickles in to cut through cheese; mayonnaise to counter bacon. It is all about the yin and the yang.

Think about texture A bit of crunch is good. Gherkins are good. Potato crisps even better.

Speed is of the essence The key to a good sandwich is to make it and eat it quickly. This isn't always possible. So if taking it to work or school, foil or greaseproof paper will keep your sandwiches fresher than clingfilm/plastic wrap, which tends to make them sweat.

Cheap bread or stale bread tastes better grilled/broiled or fried.

Cheese pretty much improves any sandwich. Especially when melted. Hot cheese is delicious. Warm lettuce is not. If you are going to toast a sandwich, omit the salad leaves.

SARDINE
sandwiches

Sardine sandwich? Fancy it? Maybe not at first, but let us try again.

Crunchy sourdough bread, toasted with half a garlic clove rubbed across its surface. A drizzle of extra-virgin olive oil. Then a tasty mix of sardines, tomatoes, capers, parsley, maybe a spot of chilli sauce if you fancy it. All snuggled underneath a gooey layer of melted mozzarella cheese.

This is delicious for a solitary lunchtime treat, made in minutes out of a mix of what you have in the fridge (parsley, chives, gherkin?) and the cupboard – a trusty tin of sardines in tomato sauce for super-fast hunger relief.

Don't assume your little ones won't like it. We know it's tempting to bring your own culinary baggage to a meal and assume that kids won't eat lentils/mackerel/sardines, but in our experience they often do. To Claire's fussy 4-year-old, sardines on toast are a treat. We know. What can we say? Go on then, here's the recipe, but it's more of a suggestion. Adapt and create with what you have in the fridge.

INGREDIENTS

2 slices of bread, sourdough or whatever you have
1 x 120g (3¾ oz) tin of sardines in tomato sauce
several flat-leaf parsley leaves, chopped
1 tbsp capers
dash of chilli sauce

black pepper
½ garlic clove
olive oil
100g (3½ oz) mozzarella cheese

Start to finish: 5 minutes

Serves: 1 greedy grown-up

Preheat the grill/broiler to high. Toast the bread.

In a bowl, mix the sardines, parsley, capers, chilli sauce and anything else you fancy. I completely break up the sardines so it is all really well mixed. Season with lots of black pepper.

Rub the garlic across the toast's surface, and drizzle the toast with olive oil.

Place the sardine mix on the toast. Shred the mozzarella over the top of the mix and pop under the grill until it melts. Devour. Lick fingers.

Sardine stats For some reason, sardines are unfashionable. They've got the same lack of glamour as corned beef, which doesn't make sense when you think about how delicious they are, how plentiful they are, and how good they are for you.

Unlike the ubiquitous tin of tuna, sardines retain all their omega-3s after the canning process; these fatty acids are good for a healthy heart. Sardines are also high in vitamin D, calcium and phosphorous, which are all good for strong bones and teeth.

And if you buy them from the Pacific Ocean – American and Canadian brands, rather than those from Mediterranean countries – you can be fairly sure that they are sustainably fished. This means the ocean bed is undamaged by their fishing methods and there is little 'bycatch', which is what happens when fishermen catch fish indiscriminately and have to throw back those they don't need, dead, into the sea. Who knew a little tin of sardines could do so much good?

SQUEAKY POCKETS
of halloumi loveliness

What child doesn't love halloumi cheese? It's the saltiness and that squeak. If you've got halloumi in the fridge (and it lasts for months in there) you know you've got a simple lunch or supper everyone will enjoy. There's no need to get complicated, but I use its saltiness as an opportunity to sneak in some deliciously charred and well-seasoned vegetables. Obviously most of them are picked out, but no one can say I don't try.

INGREDIENTS

1 courgette/zucchini
2 roasted red peppers from a jar
125g (4 oz) halloumi cheese
handful of pitted black olives
small bunch of flat-leaf parsley, chopped
4 mini pitta breads
hummus (optional)
juice of ½ lemon
salt and pepper

Start to finish: 15 minutes

Serves: 2 grown-ups or 4 children

Claire

Top and tail the courgette/zucchini, slice into thirds, and slice each third lengthways, each strip as thick as a pound coin (⅛ inch). Pop in a shallow bowl with some olive oil.

Drain the peppers from the jar. Remove any seeds and slice a bit smaller than the courgettes. Put in the same shallow bowl and make sure everything is thoroughly covered in oil.

Put a griddle pan (or a frying pan) on a high heat on the hob/ stovetop. Once it's hot, place the courgettes and peppers on the pan. Season with salt and pepper. Leave for a minute or so. Try and suppress the urge to poke about with a spatula, as this won't allow those lovely griddle lines to develop.

After a minute or so, check one of the courgettes or peppers and if they are done, turn over and cook on the other side for a minute or so. Season. Remove from pan.

Cut the halloumi into four slices 1.5cm (¼ inch) thick; at this thickness, they are less likely to fall apart. One slice will go into each pitta pocket.

Toast the pittas. Pop the halloumi in the shallow bowl and make sure the surfaces get covered in oil. Place on the hot griddle. Leave for 30-odd seconds, until griddle lines appear, and then turn. Throw in the olives for just long enough to take the chill off them.

Cut open the pittas and stuff with the courgettes, peppers, olives, chopped parsley and hot halloumi. Maybe a bit of hummus. Squeeze in some lemon juice. Eat. Squeak. Enjoy.

ROASTED ALMONDS
with rosemary

Claire

INGREDIENTS

300g (2 cups) whole
    unblanched almonds
1 tbsp salt
1 tbsp vegetable oil
1 tsp sugar
1 sprig of rosemary

Start to finish: 3 minutes prep
+ 10 minutes in the oven

A savoury snack to serve with a cold glass of wine or a beer. And perfect as an alternative to crisps/potato chips on a picnic, these roasted almonds are delicious AND adaptable. I have been known to chomp my way through a whole batch after a hard day at the parenting coalface (and where did the contents of that bottle of Sauvignon Blanc get to?).

Preheat the oven to 180°C/350°F/gas mark 4.

Lay the almonds out on a baking sheet. One by one add the salt, oil and sugar. Toss to ensure that every almond is well coated with oil and has a smattering of salt and sugar on it – I use my hands to do this. Place the sprig of rosemary over the top.

Pop in the oven for 10 minutes; remove when they are darkened and look toasted.

Let them cool, as they are kind of squeaky and chewy when still hot (and they are darn hot! Be patient!). Serve with a chilled glass of white, or with sandwiches and sunshine on a tartan picnic rug.

So, salt? I use salt. I love it. It makes most things taste better. As a family we eat very little processed food, so I can control our salt intake and don't feel bad adding it to our food. In the case of this recipe, quite a lot of salt goes into the almonds, but very little of it stays on the finished nuts, as it falls off the almonds and onto the baking sheet.

couple of small pickled gherkins
1 garlic clove
zest of ½ unwaxed lemon
500g (18 oz) steak mince/lean
    ground beef
50g (½ cup) grated Cheddar cheese
salt and pepper
olive oil

Start to finish: 10 minutes prep
+ 5 minutes cooking

Serves: 4

Burgers are unbelievably easy to make. Steak mince, salt, pepper. Bish bash bosh! Beef burger. Our ingredients list is slightly longer than this purely because we're showing off. Even so, a homemade burger takes just minutes to make and is always much better (and more trustworthy) than a shop-bought one.

Chop the gherkins, finely chop the garlic and zest the lemon. Add to the meat in a bowl together with the cheese and mix. Season well. Divide the meat into four and shape each quarter into a patty using your hands. Keep the thickest part of the burger about 2cm (¾ inch) so it cooks through properly.

Paint each patty with olive oil and then heat a griddle until really hot; you don't need to add oil. Place the patties on the griddle and cook for about 2 minutes. Use a spatula to turn the burgers and cook for another couple of minutes on the other side. They should be medium rare. Cook for longer if you like your burger more well done.

Shaping the patty Some people swear by eggs, others by breadcrumbs or putting the uncooked patty in the fridge for an hour or so to ensure the burger stays burger-shaped. Do you know what we do? Nada. It seems to work; our patties rarely crumble, and if they do they still taste good.

puddings & desserts

Nothing beats a steaming hot pudding on a cold winter's day. Or a cool, creamy pudding on a hot, sunny day. Or a tangy fruity pudding on a crisp autumn day. Basically, nothing beats pudding.

And when you're a kid – why not? It's the one time in your life you can eat pud with abandon. Cream isn't fat, it's calcium! That's not sugar, well, it's a little bit of sugar with lots of fruit! And chocolate is a great source of calories – essential when you run everywhere while flailing your arms and pretending to be a helicopter.

So as a parent, it's your duty to provide. Obviously not every day – that's what yogurt and fruit are for. But on high days and holidays, it's your duty to make fruit crumbles which make them crumble, to bake chocolate fudge puddings that ensure they won't want to leave home, ever, and to create pavlovas they measure every subsequent pavlova against for the rest of their lives. No pressure then.

Luckily it's not that hard. Really. Our selection of puds here are all life-changing, obviously, but also really, really easy and none take long to put together. Running really short of time? Check out the Ten-Second Banoffee Pie (see opposite). And most can be made from what you have in the cupboard (we're talking about you, melt-in-the-mouth pineapple crumble) and they will all make your children love you a little bit more. They are recipes for four, meaning if you're lucky, there might be a little bit left for you. Result!

TEN-SECOND *banoffee pie*

Health warning! The following recipe is lethal. Once read, there will be no turning back. It could well be your banana-geddon (groan).

Take one digestive biscuit/graham cracker, spread liberally with dulce de leche, layer on some sliced banana, top with whipped cream, sprinkle with crumbled chocolate flake (or chocolate chips) and eat. In one bite. Repeat. Banana nirvana in 10 seconds.

If you fancy something more put together, use shop-bought sweet pastry cases instead of biscuits.

Dulce du leche Exotic creature that she is, Claire lived in Argentina for a while, where she discovered dulce de leche – a spreadable caramel in a jar. When Lucy arrived after a 15-hour flight, we breakfasted on croissants smothered with it, fighting over who got to lick the knife, and we have loved it ever since. Back then (this was the late 1990s) you couldn't buy it in supermarkets and had to boil a tin of condensed milk in a pan for hours to achieve the same sticky loveliness. Now happily you can. It is delicious on ice cream.

TROPICAL CRUMBLE
with pineapple and coconut

INGREDIENTS

70g (½ cup) plain/all-purpose flour
40g (3 tbsp) cold butter
50g (¼ cup) sugar (we use light brown, but you could use any type)
40g (½ cup) desiccated/shredded coconut
50g (½ cup) tropical muesli (or normal, whatever you have)
2 x 450g (1 lb) tins of pineapple in its own juice or one large fresh pineapple

Start to finish: 10 minutes prep + 45 minutes in the oven

Serves: 4

Freezing: You can freeze the crumble mix (before you've added the muesli or coconut) in freezer bags. Just whip it out when you have the urge, add to fruit and bake.

Of course apple crumble will always be close to our hearts. We're not fickle like that. But our hearts are big, and there's room for more. Step up tropical crumble! The pineapple slowly caramelises in the oven, getting sweeter and more delicious by the minute. The fact that nothing has to be peeled or sliced for this crumble, just removed from a tin (although purists could always use fresh pineapple) means crumble just got a lot quicker.

Preheat the oven to 180°C/350°F/gas mark 4.

Rub the fridge-cold butter into the flour until it resembles breadcrumbs (see page 16 for more details on making crumble). Stir in the sugar, desiccated/shredded coconut and muesli.

Arrange the fruit (keep most of the juice back, you don't want it too sloshy) in a 1-litre (2-pint) baking dish. Spoon the crumble mix over the fruit, and lightly press it down. Bake in the oven for 45 minutes, or until the crumble is golden.

OUR MUM'S
chocolate fudge pudding

INGREDIENTS

110g (scant 1 cup) self-raising flour
55g (½ cup) cocoa powder
pinch of salt
55g (heaping ¼ cup) white sugar
110ml (scant ½ cup) milk
30g (2 tbsp) butter, melted
few drops of vanilla extract
110g (heaping ½ cup) brown sugar
170ml (¾ cup) boiling water

Start to finish: 10 minutes prep + 45 minutes in the oven

Serves: 4

This is, and always will be, our favourite family heirloom. Passed down from our mum, who found the recipe in an Australian women's magazine in the 1970s, we always have Chocolate Fudge Pudding on birthdays … and many more days besides. Even after leaving home, we frequently used to call mum asking for the recipe as did several of our friends (much to her frustration, and despite its simplicity, we never seemed to be able to write it down). Happily our children love it too, and it is now in its third generation of being a family favourite. Thanks, Mum.

Preheat the oven to 190°C/375°F/gas mark 5.

Mix the flour, half the cocoa powder, salt and white sugar into a bowl. Stir in the milk, melted butter and vanilla extract. Pour into a greased 1-litre (2-pint) ovenproof dish.

Mix together the brown sugar, remaining cocoa powder and boiling water and pour on top of the mixture in the dish. Bake for about 45 minutes. Best served with vanilla ice cream.

FROZEN *blackberry yogurt*

INGREDIENTS

450g (3 cups) fresh blackberries
1 x 400g (14 oz) tin of condensed
  milk
400g (1¾ cups) Greek yogurt

Start to finish: 5 minutes prep
+ 30 minutes in the ice-cream maker
or freezing as a lolly

Serves: 4

Who doesn't love blackberries? And when they are in abundance at certain times of the year, it's great to broaden your repertoire and step away from the crumble. We're obviously not the only one to feel like this, as this recipe is a HUGE hit on our blog and YouTube channel. It is a deliciously sweet concoction that is made in minutes. If you don't have an ice-cream maker, stick the mix in lolly (ice-cream pop) moulds instead.

First take a look at your blackberries. Make sure they are de-spidered (spiders seem to love bramble bushes!), but that's as far as we go. Washing them in water tends to bruise them and then they lose their juice.

Pop the blackberries in a blender with the condensed milk and blend. Stir in the Greek yogurt.

Pour the mix into your ice-cream maker and let it do its magic until the yogurt has frozen. Alternatively, pour into lolly moulds and put in the freezer until frozen.

Get this gadget! There are so many gizmos and gadgets out there. Some just take up valuable cupboard space (the juicer), while others would be great if we could afford them (a kitchen counter mixer, sigh!). But an ice-cream maker is the gift that keeps on giving. They are relatively cheap (the same cost as about five large tubs of expensive shop-bought ice cream) and although they do take up some space in the kitchen, they're not huge. In them you can make delicious and unusual ice-cream or sorbet/sherbet recipes from whatever you have in the fridge.

Recently, we've had kiwi, lime and coriander/cilantro sorbet (eclectic but delicious), as well as camomile, ginger and honey ice cream. Alternatively, you can go simple. Really simple. Pour in some pineapple juice, and about 40 minutes later you have homemade pineapple sorbet. Add a few mint leaves, and you have a genuinely lovely dessert, which makes your kids really happy, and costs you virtually no time and only a little money.

LEMON curd

4 unwaxed lemons, zest and juice
200g (1 cup) caster/superfine sugar
100g (7 tbsp) unsalted butter, cut into cubes
3 eggs, plus 1 extra egg yolk

Start to finish: 20 minutes

Makes: 2 jars

Historians are wrong. Ambrosia is not the food of the gods. Lemon curd is. Once you have made your own, you will never look back. It is completely different from the shop-bought stuff and although your taste buds will reap the dividends, your waistline may not. If I have a jar in the fridge, I can't pass without sneaking a spoonful. But until I made it myself, I didn't realise it contained butter. However, that is a small price to pay for happiness in a jar.

Put the lemon zest (making sure not to grate any of the bitter pith), juice, sugar and butter into a heatproof bowl. Sit the bowl over a pan of gently simmering water, making sure the water is not touching the bottom of the bowl. Stir until the butter has melted.

In a separate bowl, lightly whisk the eggs and egg yolk and stir them into the lemon mixture. Whisk until everything is mixed up and then cook over the water for 10 minutes, stirring, until the mixture thickens slightly and is creamy enough to coat the back of a spoon.

Remove from the heat and cool, stirring occasionally as it cools. I sieve mine, as I am not mad about eating zest. Also, if your eggs cook slightly by mistake, you can sieve out all the stringy bits.

Decant the curd into sterilised jars (see note on page 163). It doesn't keep for ages like jam, and is best eaten within a week.

Lucy

How to use In jam tarts, stirred through whipped cream or mascarpone to eat with cake, on spelt pancakes (page 22), in our Lemon Curd and Raspberry Cheesecake (page 184), on Cherry Pavlova (page 142) or our favourite – straight from the jar, with a finger! This is a great gift to take to a dinner party.

CASH-IT-IN *chocolate mousse*

There is never a time of the year when chocolate isn't in our lives. The gold coins of Christmas, the hearts of Valentine's Day and, of course, the eggs of Easter. After an initial gorge, we hide the remainder from children/ husbands in a cupboard and use it for cooking. We know, we are heartless. Chocolate is great in Banana Bread (page 185), Banana and Chocolate Oat Cookies (page 180) and this mousse. Although we cannot claim it is any better for children than normal chocolate, the fact we have done more than just unwrap it makes us feel marginally better. This recipe is adapted from Elizabeth David's dark chocolate version.

Break up the chocolate and melt it in a medium-sized bowl in the microwave or over a pan of simmering water, making sure the bowl doesn't touch the water. (For top tips on melting chocolate, see page 164.)

Separate the eggs and in another bowl whisk the whites into soft peaks; for speed, use an electric mixer. Add the sugar and whisk briefly.

Quickly mix the egg yolks into the bowl of melted chocolate, then whisk in a quarter of the egg white. Fold the remaining egg whites in very gently, being careful not to over-whisk, as those bubbles are precious – don't beat them out!

Pour into little sherry glasses or old-fashioned teacups and allow to set in the fridge, then decorate. We like using a biscuit or cookie as a spoon (ginger nuts/snaps are good here).

INGREDIENTS

125g (4 oz) leftover chocolate
4 eggs
4 chocolate coins/buttons/raspberries
    to decorate

Start to finish: 20 minutes

Serves: 4

CHERRY *pavlova*

Meringue
4 egg whites
250g (1¼ cups) caster/superfine
sugar

Topping
250ml (1 cup) whipping cream
1 x 400g (14 oz) tin of black
cherries, or fresh cherries, stoned

Start to finish: 15 minutes prep
+ 1–1½ hours cooking and a few
hours to cool

Serves: 6

Pavlova is one of those puddings that makes everyone eating it feel thoroughly spoilt. It is easy to bake and the tricky bit – the meringue – can be made the night before and isn't that tricky at all. Promise!

We are slightly obsessed with tinned dark cherries and have discovered they work well atop a pavlova (they are also gorgeous in a chocolate trifle or bowl of fresh custard). The juices bleed beautifully through the billows of the whipped cream. Of course, pitted fresh cherries (if you've not got a cherry stoner, they are worth the money) would be lovely too.

We posted a similar pavlova recipe a couple of years ago on our blog and just presumed that readers would know not to assemble it until just before eating, as the meringue would dissolve. One didn't and took us to task.

Preheat the oven to 150°C/300°F/gas mark 2.

Using a pencil, mark out the circumference of a dinner plate on baking paper. Put it on a baking sheet, pencil marking side down.

Whisk the egg whites with an electric mixer until they form stiff peaks, then whisk in the sugar, 1 tbsp at a time, until the meringue looks glossy and thick.

Spread the meringue inside the circle, creating a crater by making the sides a little higher than the middle. Bake for 1–1½ hours, then turn off the heat and let the pavlova cool completely inside the oven. This is important, otherwise it will be soggy, not gooey.

Just before serving, whip the cream into soft peaks and gently spread over the meringue, piling it into the centre and spreading it outwards. Then pile on the cherries. If you are using tinned ones, you will have to drain them first (but keep all that delicious syrup – you can either serve it in a jug alongside the pavlova or drink it yourself). Residual cherry juice will dribble through the cream, creating a Gothic masterpiece. A pavlova fit for a vampire.

A few rules

- Eggs should be at room temperature.

- Make sure there is no yolk in the whites (we like using cartoned egg whites) and the bowl should be spotlessly clean or the eggs won't form stiff peaks.

- This is not one of those recipes where you can play around with the ingredients. Caster/superfine sugar is a must.

FLAMBÉED bananas

30g (2 tbsp) unsalted butter
2 tbsp brown sugar
1 banana, sliced lengthways
rum (if you don't have any,
    rifle through your drinks
    cupboard. Most fruity,
    non-creamy spirits work,
    although they must have
    a high alcohol content,
    otherwise it won't burst
    into flame)

Start to finish: 5 minutes

Serves: 1

Once upon a time, flambéed bananas were considered the height of sophistication. Now, they are so out of vogue, they sound more like a dubious act between consenting adults than a once-popular dessert. Which is a shame, because they are delicious and you get to set fire to them. Bonus! The only note of caution is… watch your eyebrows.

Melt the butter in a frying pan, add the sugar and cook on a low heat until it is melted. Slowly lower the banana into the caramelly liquid. It will smell gorgeous, but don't touch – it is hot! Cook for a couple of minutes, turning once. We find it easier to do this with tongs; that way the bananas don't break. When it looks done (browned, sticky, soft) take it off the heat. Then throw in your rum.

Using a long match, light the pan. Stand back, quickly. The flames burn most of the alcohol off. When they've died down, serve with vanilla ice cream. If you are serving this to your children, you may want to hold off the alcohol!

SLOW-ROASTED strawberries

INGREDIENTS

1kg (2¼ lb) strawberries
1 tbsp sugar
2 tbsp balsamic vinegar

Start to finish: 10 minutes prep
+ 1 hour in the oven

Serves: 4 grown-ups

Slow-roasted strawberries? Are we crazy? Stay with us as these are amazing. Think caramelised, think jammy, think easy. Obviously, we love a strawberry as raw and naked as the day it was picked, but for a transformation we slow roast. Perfect when strawberries aren't in their prime, it transports pale out-of-season red bullets or disguises the fact that they are a bit past it. Eat with Greek yogurt for pudding, on muesli for breakfast or with a spoon because you're peckish.

Preheat the oven to 160°C/325°F/gas mark 3.

Line a baking sheet with baking paper (you don't have to, but it stops any charred bits of last Sunday's roast getting involved) and pop the washed and hulled strawberries on top.

Sprinkle over the sugar and vinegar, then use your hands to mix the whole lot up, so the strawberries are well covered. Make sure the strawberries aren't all on top of each other, but are well separated, so they roast rather than stew – you may need two baking sheets. Pop in the oven for an hour, maybe giving each strawberry a little nudge or turn after 40 minutes. When removed from the oven, you want the syrup to be gloopy, not dry.

Let them cool for a little bit. Use a silicone spatula to give the entire base of the baking sheet a scrape, which results in the recovery of a surprising amount of syrup. Pop in the fridge until you're ready to eat, or just eat.

PEACH *and cherry cobbler*

INGREDIENTS

500g (18 oz) tinned peaches, drained
150g (1 cup) frozen cherries
150g (1 heaping cup) plain/all-
    purpose flour
150g (¾ cup) caster/superfine sugar
pinch of salt
1 egg, beaten
90g (¾ stick) butter, melted

Start to finish: 10 minutes prep
+ 30–40 minutes in the oven

Serves: 4

To make this recipe you must rise early in the morn' and pluck the peaches and cherries from the fruit trees in your garden. What? You don't have any? Never fear, this recipe is just as good with a tin of peaches and some frozen cherries. It takes a few minutes to make and your kids will love you forever.

Preheat the oven to 180°C/350°F/gas mark 4.

Drain the syrup from the peaches; you don't need it, although it is delicious to drink. Place the peaches and cherries in a 20-cm (8-inch) round cake pan. You don't need to grease it.

Put the flour, sugar and salt in a bowl. Stir in the egg and melted butter. When it is well-mixed, spoon the 'cobbler' over the fruit mix. It should be uneven and not necessarily cover all the filling.

Place in the oven and bake for 30–40 minutes, until golden. Serve with crème fraîche, custard or ice cream.

Flavours The great thing about this dish is you can make it with loads of different fruits, and you can use tinned or frozen when there's not much fresh about. Tinned or fresh rhubarb is divine (scatter a lot of sugar over the rhubarb if it's fresh; you won't need it if it's tinned). Frozen berries are yum, or try fresh gooseberries drizzled with Elderflower Cordial, page 163.

Claire

child's play

Whilst we agree the idea of cooking with your children is often more appealing than the reality, it is a great way to spend an afternoon and pique their interest in food. Research shows if you involve children in cooking, they are more likely to cook as adults. You thought you were just making cupcakes? Nope, you're saving them from a life of ready meals.

This chapter contains recipes that you can make with your children or that slightly older ones can make on their own. Some are sweet, but there a few savoury dishes too. The butter and ice cream recipes involve a lot of shaking so are part magic, part science lesson and part bicep workout. Nothing beats baking your own bread and our recipe is pretty much kid-proof. Edible piñatas – what can we say? Make them, smash them, eat them. They are great for playdates and parties. But our ultimate favourite – and perhaps yours too, judging by its popularity on our YouTube channel – is Five-minute Cake-in-a-cup. The title tells you all you need to know.

If you have teenagers, many of the book's recipes are easy to make with only a little guidance. Teach them well enough and before long, it could be like having that private live-in chef you've always dreamed of, albeit one who draws the line at doing the washing up.

BANANA *ice cream*

INGREDIENTS

1 banana

Optional extras
chocolate hazelnut spread
dates
honey
peanut butter
ground cinnamon

Start to finish: Overnight
to freeze banana
+ 3 minutes to whizz up

Serves: 1

Make this and watch magic happen. One minute you have a banana. The next you have a creamy, cool ice cream. Jaws will drop. Children will think you have special powers. Make this with them when they have a playdate and suddenly you become Supermum.

Freeze your banana (do the chopped option below) until it is really hard.

Pop the frozen banana chunks in a shallow bowl. Using a hand-held blender, blend. Blend. Then blend again. Stop the blender occasionally and use a spatula to push the ice cream mixture down off the sides of the blender. Then blend some more. Add any additional flavourings you fancy and give a last blend. Serve.

How to freeze a banana Um, stick it in the freezer. Really, it's that simple. There is an argument for peeling it first (easier to peel defrosted than when frozen). And there is another argument for chopping it into chunks first (it will take up less room). But really the only thing you actually need to do is pop it in a freezer bag. Once frozen, your banana is a blank canvas. Dip it into melted chocolate for a luxurious lolly/ice-cream pop. Or just stick it into the banana bread you didn't have a chance to make earlier in the week …

SHAKE YOUR OWN *ice cream*

INGREDIENTS

lots of ice cubes
6 tbsp salt
120ml (½ cup) milk
1 tbsp sugar
¼ tsp vanilla extract
chocolate chips or chopped
    fresh fruit
large plastic zip bag
medium plastic zip bag
gloves!

Start to finish: 5–10 minutes

Serves: 2

Using just your biceps and a few ingredients, you can make ice cream in 5 minutes. Did we say you won't need a freezer? Or an ice-cream maker? If that sounds like magic … it is.

Put the ice and salt in the large bag, about half filling it with ice. Pour the milk, sugar and vanilla into the medium bag, expel the air and seal it. Bury the medium bag in the ice of the large bag and seal the large bag. Shake vigorously for 5 minutes. The bags will be cold so wear gloves.

Have a squeeze and if the milk has thickened, you have your ice cream. When fairly solid, remove the medium bag from the large bag and wipe off the salty water. Open the medium bag and decorate with chocolate chips or fruit. Eat straight from the bag.

The science bit Apparently turning milk into ice cream isn't just a wondrous form of magic, there is a scientific explanation for it. Here goes: for milk to turn into ice cream, it has to lose heat. Ice absorbs this heat. The salt makes it better at doing this. How? Adding salt makes the ice colder as it lowers the ice's freezing point. This means it can absorb more heat than normal ice, giving it the power to freeze the milk. Got that?

Claire

FIVE-MINUTE
cake-in-a-cup

This cake is so dangerous, it even has its own Facebook page warning that you are only 5 minutes away from chocolate cake at any time of day or night. And it's true. Take a look. You've probably got all the ingredients in your cupboard. Next thing you know, they're in a cup, in the microwave, in your mouth. Bang! You're eating chocolate cake. For additional danger, watch the cake cook in the microwave. It rises and rises until you're sure it's going to explode … normally it doesn't. This is our most popular YouTube recipe of all time.

Mix the dry ingredients together in a large bowl. Add the egg and mix thoroughly. Pour in the milk and oil and mix well.

Add the chocolate chips and vanilla extract, and mix again. Divide the mixture between the two teacups.

Put the teacups in the microwave one at a time and cook for 60 seconds at 1000 watts (high) or until risen and cooked. Allow to cool a little and serve with natural yogurt (an attempt at being healthy) or ice cream.

INGREDIENTS

4 tbsp self-raising flour
4 tbsp sugar
2 tbsp cocoa powder
1 egg
3 tbsp milk
3 tbsp oil (I use sunflower; melted butter would probably be nicer, but it would take too long, and the idea of this recipe is that it is quick)
3 tbsp chocolate chips (or just smash up a bar of chocolate)
a small splash of vanilla extract
2 teacups or small mugs to cook the cake

Start to finish: Um, 5 minutes

Serves: 2

Playdate fun Rather than make this yourself, find lots of little people to help you. This is great playdate entertainment. Each child mixes their own cake and then watches it nearly explode in the microwave. Not many desserts provide this level of excitement.

CHEESY *stars*

INGREDIENTS

225g (1¾ cups) Cheddar cheese, grated
60g (½ stick) butter, softened
125g (1 scant cup) plain/all-purpose flour
pinch of salt
a splash of water
a shaking of smoked paprika to garnish (optional)
5g (1 heaping tbsp) grated Parmesan cheese (optional)

Start to finish: 10 minutes prep + 10 minutes in the oven

Makes: 20 medium-sized stars

This is a starry variation of good old cheese straws. Kids love eating them and making them. Older ones can weigh the ingredients and form the dough; younger ones can be set free with the cookie cutters.

Preheat the oven to 200°C/400°F/gas mark 6 and grease or line two baking sheets.

In a large bowl, stir the Cheddar and butter together until well mixed. Add the flour and salt and stir well. By now, the mix is probably looking like chunky breadcrumbs. Add a splash of water and use your hands to pull the dough together. The heat of your hands should make this a little easier. If you need to, add a little more water.

Sprinkle some flour on the work surface, and put the lump of dough on top. Roll it out until it is just under 1cm (½ inch) thick. Use a star-shaped cookie cutter to stamp out the shapes until there is no dough left, re-rolling the scraps as necessary.

Place the stars on the baking sheets, and sprinkle the paprika and Parmesan over the top, if using. Pop in the oven for 10–12 minutes, until they are golden brown and the house smells deliciously cheesy. Cool on a wire rack.

COCONUT *macaroons*

INGREDIENTS

2 egg whites
100g (½ cup) caster/superfine sugar
160g (2 heaping cups) desiccated/shredded coconut

Start to finish: 5 minutes + 15 minutes in the oven

Makes: 12

Ever had one of those mornings when, mildly hungover, you find the cupboard completely bare of anything except some eggs and desiccated/shredded coconut? Just us, then? Every cloud has a silver lining, as that was how these delicious, easy to make, bite-sized cookies were discovered. Little, chewy and sweet, they are easy enough for children to make with very little supervision. Hungover adults, too!

Preheat the oven to 180°C/350°F/gas mark 4. Grease or line a baking sheet,

With a spoon, mix the egg whites, sugar and coconut in a bowl. Nope, you haven't misread the recipe. The egg whites don't need to be whipped first; they go in with everything else as they are.

Empty the mixture onto a worktop and press it down with your hands until you have a square-ish shape about 1cm (½ inch) high. Use a small cookie cutter or glass (about 4cm/1½ inches wide) and cut out rounds.

Place them on the baking sheet and bake for 12–15 minutes until golden. Cool on a wire rack.

BAKE-THEM-YOURSELF
decorations

250g (1 cup) salt (not sea salt! You want the cheap fine stuff)

130g (1 cup) plain/all-purpose flour

¼ tsp essential oil (such as lavender) to make the dough smell delicious (optional)

a splash of food colouring to change the dough's colour (optional)

120ml (½ cup) water

Start to finish: 5 minutes to make the salt dough, hours to shape it, 3 hours in the oven, or allow to air dry overnight above a radiator

Makes: 10 decorations, depending on size

Computer consoles come and go, but salt dough will always be there. We remember it from our own childhood, and now, when it rains or it's a wintry half term, out come the salt and flour, on goes the oven, and hours – ok, minutes – of fun is had, making these. And for the record, salt dough is not edible.

Mix the salt and flour in a large bowl. Add the essential oil and food colouring, if using. Gradually add the water – you may not need it all. When the mixture looks doughy, knead it on a floured surface until it's smooth, not sticky.

Roll it out with a rolling pin – you want it pretty thin, less than 1cm (½ inch), to stop your decorations from being too hefty. Use cookie cutters as you would normally. A straw is useful for making a hole at the top of the decoration, to thread ribbon through.

Preheat the oven to 100°C/225°F/gas mark ¼.

Place the decorations on baking paper on a baking sheet and put in the oven for about 3 hours. When the decorations are baked, let them cool and then paint. A layer of PVA glue with some glitter thrown on gives them a pretty finish.

Inspiration Use the right cookie cutters and you've got the perfect Christmas tree decorations. Beautiful ribbon for hanging and a sprinkling of good-quality glitter can transform your two-year-old's attempts at art into something quite tasteful.

You can be really creative and use salt dough as a way to record your growing family. A tiny foot or hand imprint can capture a moment in time. Family fingerprints on a circle look like a Christmas bauble. Obviously a certain amount of artistic flair is helpful with all this. But if an afternoon with the salt dough just leaves you with a floury splodge, rather than something you want to put on Pinterest (where there are millions of great ideas), that's all right too. No one minds, least of all your 4-year-old.

EDIBLE *piñata*

1 ice cream cone – the waffle patterned ones are best, about 4cm (1½ inches) wide at the top

squirty can of icing (or icing/ confectioners' sugar and water to make your own)

sprinkles

edible glitter and other bling

handful of small unwrapped sweets/candies, small enough to fit inside the cone

1 small meringue, about 4cm (1½ inches) wide

Start to finish: If you are making them, 5 minutes each, max. If your children are, 15 minutes.

Makes: 1

Hands up if 10 years ago you knew what a piñata was? An exotic sounding cocktail? A Voodoo doll? A new waxing technique? The answer is, of course, a papier mâché figure filled with sweets and toys. These days, no children's party is complete without this Mexican celebratory tradition. It is no surprise they are a hit – quite literally – as they involve sweets and violence – you have to smash the suspended figure, blindfolded, with a stick to release the goodies inside. This slightly less aggressive DIY version is a great playdate activity.

Take the ice-cream cone and decorate with sprinkles and edible glitter, using the icing as a kind of glue. We like to write our initials on the side. (If you don't want your children's fingers to get too sticky, leave the cones clear.) Once your cone is a masterpiece, fill it up with sweets and candies.

Squirt icing (of course you can make your own using icing/ confectioners' sugar and water, but the squirty canned icing you can buy in large supermarkets lasts ages and is fun to use) inside the cone's rim and carefully fit the meringue on top. It is like they are made for each other.

As you are going to smash the cone eventually, it may seem self-defeating to rest it carefully inside a glass or something similar until the icing dries, but this is what we are going to suggest.

When dry, smash and eat.

Grown-up version Turn these into a grown-up treat by making your own meringues, covering the cones in melted chocolate and chopped pistachios, and filling them with posh chocolate chunks. It makes a change from after-dinner mints.

A clever way to display these is by taking an ordinary shallow box, covering the sides in wrapping paper, fixing cardboard over the top and punching an individual hole for each piñata.

500g (4 cups) strong white bread flour
7g (2 tsp) fast-action dried yeast/ active dry yeast
10g (2 tsp) salt
50ml (scant ¼ cup) olive oil
300ml (1¼ cups) tepid water

Start to finish: about 3½ hours on and off (of which only about 30 minutes is prep as the rest is waiting for the dough to rise) + 35 minutes in the oven.

Makes: 1 large loaf

As we all know, nothing is really kiddie proof, but this is as near as bread gets. This dough will withstand pretty much whatever your children throw at it. The only thing I ask is that you ensure their fingernails are clean before they start, because after 10 minutes kneading they will be spotless (unlike the dough...).

Stir the flour, yeast and salt together in a big bowl, so it's well mixed. Make a well in the centre of the flour. Pour in the olive oil and most of the water.

Flick the flour from the outside in, to cover the yeast water as this will stop your hands getting quite so mucky. Then start kneading inside the bowl. If it's too dry, add more water until you get the right consistency.

Once the dough has come together, start kneading on the worktop. Use a small amount of oil or flour to stop it sticking, but not too much as it will change the consistency of the dough.

Knead for about 10 minutes. Almost throw the dough in front of you, then pull it back – you should see the elastic strands of the gluten as you pull it back. Quarter turn the dough and do the same thing again. Keep on going for about 10 minutes.

When it's done, put it in an oiled bowl and place a damp tea/dish towel over the top. Wait for it to 'prove' – a process that lasts until the dough has doubled in size. Do it in a hot kitchen, and it will happen quickly. But if you don't want the bread until the next morning, prove it in the fridge overnight. It will still double in size, but will take longer.

Grease a 900g (9 x 5 inch) loaf tin. Preheat the oven to 230°C/ 450°F/gas mark 8.

When the dough has proven, you need to 'knock it back'. This is just a bit of punching, about two minutes worth, to get the air out of the dough, compared to the heavy-duty kneading of earlier.

Turn the dough into a ball and knock it into a long rounded shape, which will fit in the loaf tin. Pop it in and let it prove again, uncovered, until it has doubled in size. Cut the top with a serrated knife and place in the hot oven.

After about 35 minutes, remove from the oven using a clean tea/dish towel. Take the bread out of the tin, hold it upside down and give it a sharp tap – it should sound hollow. If it is, remove it from the oven, take it out of the tin (you don't want it to steam) and let it cool properly on a wire rack.

Claire

Making bread with kids How much breadmaking you can do with your kids depends on their ages. Older kids can measure; younger ones can stir. Kneading is a bit trickier. You want the bread to be properly kneaded, but small hands probably can't do it effectively. So play this game with them:

Sitting at a clean, lightly floured table, set your timer for 10 minutes. Then whack the bread down in front of you and give it a flamboyant knead. Pass the dough to your child. Let them knead, and with rhythmic, almost military timing, shout 'pass the dough!' sporadically. They then have to slap the dough down hard in front of the next person. This is obviously more fun with more kids, but I confess it's actually quite fun with one kid and one adult. Keep going until the timer goes off.

Shaping the bread can also be a fun part of the process. Once the dough has been 'knocked back' you can take half to be cooked into something edible by you, and they can shape the rest. We've made little rolls, seeded cottage loaves and plaits/braids, some with more success than others!

The science bit What makes bread rise? Yeast. It's a single cell fungi that eats sugar and burps out alcohol and carbon dioxide gas. The carbon dioxide gives bread its 'airy' texture – all those air holes. The alcohol helps give bread some of its flavour. How does dough actually grow? When wheat flour and water are kneaded, they create a really stretchy substance called gluten. This captures all those air bubbles which means the bread expands in size.

INGREDIENTS

500ml (2 cups) double/heavy cream
2 x jam jars, sterilised (see page 163)

Start to finish: hmmmm, depends how vigorously you shake. About 15 minutes. Less if you cheat and use a food mixer – but where is the fun in that?

Makes: 2 pats

Top tip If you want to use a food mixer and give your muscles a break, then you can do the shaking with your beater attachment.

DIY *butter*

When we were little, we made our own butter in jam jars at our Auntie's house. It seemed like magic at the time, and still does now. All you have to do is shake, shake, shake and watch liquid cream turn to butter. Abracadabra!

Divide the cream between the jars and start shaking. That is all you do. For ages. Arms hurting yet? Eventually you will see some clumps separate from the cream. This is butter. Eventually, the pats of butter will get bigger, although there will still be some liquid in the jar. This liquid is buttermilk. You can use it in the recipes on pages 22 and 186.

Open the jars and, with your (clean) hands, squeeze as much liquid as you can out of the butter. Then put both pats in a clean sieve and allow to drain. Alternatively, put them in a muslin cloth/cheesecloth and squeeze. Take a bowl of ice-cold water and submerge the butter, kneading it while it is still in the water to get rid of any remaining pesky bits of buttermilk. Kneading butter may sound odd, but if you don't, the butter will be sour. Empty the bowl and start again with clean ice-cold water. Do this until the water runs clear, about 2–3 times.

Drain the butter. If you want it salted, put it in a bowl and knead 2 tsp of sea salt through it. Put it in a suitably sized pot and store in the fridge. All you need now is some hot bread – see opposite page.

MARZIPAN *fruit*

Lucy

As children, making marzipan fruit heralded the start of Christmas. We would spend hours dyeing marzipan red, yellow and green and then rolling it into tiny balls to make bunches of grapes, apples and oranges, using cloves for stalks. Our fruit baskets were given pride of place on the sideboard, where they would gather dust for weeks before eventually being thrown away. No one actually ate them. Mum probably warned people how they had been made. It was huge fun and something we both do now with our children. They love it and judging by how popular our Marzipan Fruit video is on YouTube, you do too.

INGREDIENTS

2 x 500g (2¼ lb) packs of
    marzipan (white if possible)
food colouring pastes – red,
    blue, yellow, black (NB pastes
    make richer colours than
    liquid food colouring, but
    both work well)
toothpicks
whole cloves
cheese graters
edible glitter (optional)

Start to finish: how long is
a piece of string?

Makes: enough for 8 children
(perfect for playdates/
Christmas party activity)

This is incredibly easy, but there are a few tricks that make it even easier.

It's probably best that you, rather than your children, actually dye the marzipan. This avoids covering the whole house in food colouring, as well as dyeing your children's fingers for weeks. To colour marzipan you take a tiny spot of colouring on a toothpick and knead it into the marzipan with your fingers until it is a uniform colour. Keep adding colour until it is the shade you are looking for.

You mix marzipan just like paint. So red and blue marzipan kneaded together makes purple, blue and yellow is green and so on. This means you don't need to buy every colour. Just the primary colours should do the trick, although black is handy, especially for watermelon seeds. I make more yellow and less black as I always use more yellow, while black is mostly used for details.

I give each child a plate with portions of different coloured marzipan on it. Then let them run riot. It is just edible play dough really.

Gently pushing a grater (using the smallest holes) into the marzipan makes it look like orange and lemon peel or strawberry seeds. My favourite fruits to make are mini watermelon slices complete with black seeds, rosy red apples with cloves as stalks and bunches of dark purple grapes. Toothpicks make good tools to sculpt with. Edible glitter can be rubbed into the marzipan to give it a nice sheen.

Don't confine yourself to fruit either. This year, we made old-fashioned plum puddings, brightly coloured Christmas presents with bows and even a Christmas tree with baubles. One little boy who visited made a monster and a football. Clearly, the only limit is your imagination.

CHAPTER 13

drinks

We know you really like experimenting with drinks because whenever we write about them, you go bonkers. Our Blackberry Brandy recipe (see page 160) is one of our most popular blog posts and YouTube videos ever. You clearly all have good taste... or maybe just drink a lot.

Actually, it is not just booze that gets you going. One of our most read blog posts ever was on tasty, but alcohol-free drinks that don't leave non-drinkers feeling uncherished. Teetotallers really pull the short straw when it comes to quality and choice. So next time you have one for dinner (or are indeed one yourself), you can pull out all the stops and pamper them with our Ginger and Lime Cordial (see page 162) or an Affogato (see page 163).

We have summer coolers (Childhood Lemonade, see page 161) and winter warmers (Warm Spiced Apple Juice, see page 160) and there is even a recipe for ice cubes. Yes, you read that correctly. A recipe! For ice cubes! It is slightly more involved than it sounds. Well, sort of. Intrigued?

RAINBOW *ice cubes*

Children love cocktails. Not the alcoholic sort obviously, that would be illegal, but anything garishly coloured with curly straws and lots of ice. These two ice cube recipes are perfect. Yes, that's correct, a recipe for ice cubes. Are you paying attention? It's complicated.*

Coloured ice cubes Fill ice cube trays (you could use different shaped ice cubes too) with different coloured fruit juices. Cranberry and orange work well together, but think what colours look good together as well as flavours. Freeze until solid. Put lots of different coloured cubes in a glass and pour over cold lemonade. Straw and cocktail umbrella obligatory!

Flower ice cubes In an ice cube tray place a clean tiny sprig of lavender, an edible flower petal (like a rose or nasturtium) or herb leaf (mint is nice). Top with water. Freeze. They look so beautiful, like mini glaciers. The mint cubes are lovely in iced tea, with a rum cocktail or simply with water and slices of lemon.

*Joke

PEACH *melba smoothie*

INGREDIENTS

1 x 400g (14 oz) tin of peach halves in juice
150g (scant 1 cup) frozen raspberries
200ml (scant 1 cup) apple juice

Start to finish: 2 minutes

Serves: 2

This is a smoothie for when it is cold outside and fresh fruits are few and far between. Although we have used tinned peaches and frozen raspberries, it is just as good with fresh fruit. Perfect when you need a vitamin – and sunshine – injection. Our children love making and drinking this and it is a great breakfast, as you pack in two of your five-a-day before you've even left the house.

Pour the peaches, juice and all, into a blender. Add the raspberries and apple juice. Blitz until smooth. Drink.

BANANA, KIWI *and almond smoothie*

INGREDIENTS

2 bananas
2 kiwi fruit (peel this with a vegetable peeler and cut off the ends)
2 glasses almond milk (this is lactose-free)

Start to finish: 2 minutes

Serves: 2

Smoothies are a gorgeous way to start the day. They are also a great way to encourage children to try different fruits – like the kiwi fruit or hairy egg as it is affectionately known round our way.

Whizz up all the ingredients in a blender until smooth and drink.

Claire

BLACKBERRY *brandy*

There's only a limited amount of crumble any adult should consume. And in autumn, when apples abound and blackberries literally fall into your basket, a LOT of crumble goes down. Which is why you shouldn't feel bad about taking nature's bounty, possibly picked by your child's chubby little hands, and turning it into alcohol. Especially when it's alcohol that tastes this delicious. So forget about crumble, compote and the kids. Stick your blackberries in some brandy and congratulate yourself on this early investment in a merry Christmas!

(see page 163)

INGREDIENTS

1 750ml (25 fl oz) glass bottle with lid or stopper, sterilised (see page 163)
400g (about 3 cups) blackberries, enough to fill the bottle two-thirds full
700ml (scant 3 cups) mid-range brandy (doesn't need to be expensive, just don't get something which is so cheap, it will give you a horrible hangover!)
85g (scant ½ cup) white sugar, approximately

Start to finish: 5 minutes

Makes: 750ml (25 fl oz)

You could wash the blackberries, but this does damage them a bit. I'd just pick through them, removing any dead blossoms or insects.

Put the empty bottle on some digital scales and re-set the monitor so it reads 0g/0 oz. Fill the bottle two-thirds full of blackberries. How much do those blackberries weigh? Then for some maths. For each 400g/14 oz of fruit, you need to add 85g/scant ½ cup of sugar. Work out how much sugar that is for you and then add it to the bottle. Fill the rest of the bottle with brandy, and seal with the lid.

See? Easy. Give the bottle an occasional shake once a week or so. Then wait, ideally until Christmas.

Let me count the ways this drink can perk up your evening.
* Pop a brandy-sozzled blackberry in the bottom of a champagne glass. Add sparkly stuff. Drink.
* Pop a small amount of brandy in a champagne glass. Add sparkly stuff. Drink.
* Go camping. Get really, really cold. Remember you packed blackberry brandy. Perk up. Drink. Really, the list is endless.

Warm Spiced Apple Juice Brrr! Baby, it's cold outside and this is the ultimate child-friendly (and teetotal) winter warmer. Simply take a litre (quart) of apple juice (cloudy is best) and warm it in a saucepan with a few strips of orange peel and a cinnamon stick for 5 minutes, to allow flavours to infuse. Pour into mugs and warm yourself up. Who needs mittens?

PS Add a dash of rum and you have a different drink entirely, equally delicious, but perhaps not one for the kids.

Lucy

CHILDHOOD *lemonade*

There is something delightful about making your own lemonade. It tastes so much better than anything shop-bought and you feel like you've stepped from the pages of an Enid Blyton book. I used to make lemonade with our mum as a little girl and now I make it with my children. This is a cordial, meant for diluting, but nonetheless, when you make your own, you cannot deny how much sugar it contains, so take a deep breath …

INGREDIENTS

2 unwaxed lemons
600g (3 cups) caster/superfine sugar
1 litre (1 quart) water
20g (¾ oz) citric acid (available online or from chemists or pharmacies)

Start to finish: 10 minutes prep + 12 hours steeping

Makes: about 1.5 litres (3¼ pints) of cordial which you dilute to taste

Grate the zest of the lemons into a big heatproof bowl. Avoid the white pith, as it tastes 'bleugh' and will ruin the flavour. Once grated, take a small sharp knife and cut the ends off the lemons so they stand firm on the worktop. Then slice down removing as much pith as possible. It is worth investing a little time in this.

Next slice the lemon fruit thinly and add to the bowl with the sugar and a litre (quart) of boiling water. There is something rather lovely about the lemons bobbing about. Stir gently until all the sugar is dissolved.

Leave to steep overnight. The next day dissolve the citric acid in 100ml (scant ½ cup) water, add to the mixture and stir again. This puts the zing back into it, allowing you to taste the lemon and not just sugar.

Sieve the cordial into a clean jug and store in the fridge for up to a week. Dilute to taste with still or sparkling water. Decorate with basil or mint leaves for a twist.

INGREDIENTS

500ml (2 cups) cider
zest of ½ orange
3cm (1¼ inch) piece of fresh ginger root, peeled and chopped into about 4 pieces
seeds of 2 cardamom pods
1 cinnamon stick
1 tbsp sugar

Start to finish: 10 minutes + 24 hours steeping

Makes: 4 small glasses

MULLED *cider*

There are few events, in winter especially, which aren't improved by a thermos of mulled cider. It makes Bonfire Night go with a bang, the shrieks of trick or treating at Halloween seem more mellow, and an afternoon at the supermarket feel almost fun. Have I gone too far?

Pour the cider into a saucepan. Add the orange zest, ginger, cardamom seeds, cinnamon stick and sugar. Turn the heat up and bring to the boil. Turn off the heat and let it steep for 10 minutes. Pour. Drink.

GINGER AND LIME
cordial

INGREDIENTS

1 big chunk of ginger root
zest and juice of 1 large unwaxed
    lemon
zest and juice of 2 limes
sugar, to taste
Tabasco sauce

Start to finish: 5 minutes prep
+ 30 minutes cooking
+ steeping time

Makes: 600ml (2½ cups)

Non-alcoholic beverages for grown-ups don't seem to have evolved since the 1970s. The choice is lemonade or cola, which is fine if you want to jump head first into a vat of sugar, but not so fine if you fancy something a bit special. Luckily we've discovered this cordial – easy to make at home, what it lacks in alcohol it makes up for in taste. If you want something the kids will enjoy, just make it slightly sweeter.

Peel the ginger and cut into fairly thin chunks and put in a saucepan. Add the lemon and lime zest, some sugar – maybe a tablespoon or so at this point – and 600ml or so (2½ cups) of boiling water.

Bring back to the boil and simmer for 30 minutes, then take off the heat, add the lime and lemon juice and a generous hit of Tabasco, and adjust the sugar levels if you want. Leave to steep until it's cool, then strain into a bottle.

This cordial mixes up really well with fizzy water (and rum if you're not teetotal), but give the bottle a good shake before you pour. It will keep for a week in the fridge, but chances are it won't last that long.

MINT *cordial*

INGREDIENTS

bunch of fresh mint leaves
juice of 2 lemons
500g (2½ cups) sugar
300ml (1¼ cups) water

Start to finish: 5 minutes prep
+ steeping time

Makes: 300ml (1¼ cups)

Really good for zooshing up fruit juices; particularly good with orange or pineapple, or both.

Give the mint leaves a good bash in a pestle and mortar until they're pulpy. Put into a heatproof bowl, then stir in the lemon juice and leave to stand for 1 hour.

Make a syrup by boiling 2 parts sugar and 1 part water together, then pour it, still boiling, over the leaves and lemon. When slightly cooled, taste for sweetness, steep until cold, then strain. Add to fruit juice.

1 double espresso coffee
sugar, to taste
a large glass of ice

Start to finish: 1 minute

Serves: 1

CAFÉ *con hielo*

Thank you to the Spanish, for rescuing us from cola as the only source of caffeine on a hot day. Coffee becomes a creature of exquisite subtlety and fragrance consumed this way.

Take your hot espresso and sweeten it the way you like it. Pour it over the ice. Yes, really, that's all. You'll be amazed.

2 scoops vanilla ice cream
1 very hot espresso

Start to finish: 2 minutes

Serves: 1

AFFOGATO

Technically not a drink, of course, but so simple and so delicious that you almost don't miss the dessert wine everyone else is enjoying.

Put your ice cream into a tall glass. Pour over the espresso. Eat with a spoon until you get to the point where you can simply drink the dregs.

1.3kg (6½ cups) sugar
flowers from 15–20 elderflower heads
    (ideally picked when they are at
    their prime and on a hot day)
2 oranges
3 lemons
30g (1 oz) citric acid (available from
    the chemist/pharmacy)
muslin or cheesecloth

Start to finish: 20 minutes
+ 24 hours steeping

Makes: 2 x 750ml (2 x 25 oz)
bottles (wine bottles are ideal)

To sterilise bottles, stick them on a wash at the top of the dishwasher. Alternatively wash them normally, leave a little wet and blitz in the microwave for 45 seconds. The old-fashioned way is to put them in a low, low oven for 20 minutes. Take care when removing them as they will be hot! Wait until the bottles have cooled before filling them.

ELDERFLOWER *cordial*

Claire first made this on holiday in Cornwall. She came back from a walk brimming with freshly-picked elderflowers and in a recreation of television's *The Good Life*, proceeded to make a vat of fragrant cordial. We have been hooked ever since and make it every year, as soon as the flowers are in bloom.

Put the sugar in a large pan with 1 litre (5 cups) of water. Heat until the sugar dissolves and only then bring to the boil. Add the flower heads (which you've already shaken to remove any insects) and bring to the boil again. As soon as it is boiling, remove from the heat.

Thinly slice the fruit and put in a large bowl or jug. Add the citric acid and pour over the hot syrup and flowers. Stir well and cover loosely with muslin or cheesecloth. Leave for 24 hours.

Sterilise the bottles (see left). Strain the liquid through the muslin into another bowl or jug. Funnel into the bottles.

Nicest diluted with fizzy water or sparkling wine. A sprig of rosemary works as a garnish. Elderflower cordial is also wonderful in sorbets/sherbets, granitas and trifles.

spoons

100g (3½ oz) plain/semisweet chocolate
15g (2 heaping tbsp) cocoa powder
30g (¼ cup) icing/confectioners' sugar

Decorations
sprinkles, popping candy, mini-marshmallows

Equipment
silicone ice cube tray
8 light teaspoons – plastic ones are good. Alternatively, use drinking straws or cocktail umbrellas for additional impact!

Start to finish: 20 minutes + 1–2 hours in the fridge

Makes: 8 spoons

Hot chocolate is the ultimate treat in Claire's house. Ask the 4-year-old what he'd like most in the world, and despite blazing sunshine and the thermometer hitting scorchio, he will always answer 'hot chocolate and marshmallows'. These chocolate spoons provide both, plus they look great. Serve at a playdate or small party so the children can impress their friends.

Melt the chocolate (see below). Once melted, stir in the icing/confectioners' sugar and cocoa. Spoon the mixture into a silicone ice cube tray. If it's a bit uneven or messy on the top, use a palette or butter knife to scrape away the untidy bits. Stick the spoons in the chocolate. Scatter the chocolate with the decorations. Place the tray in the fridge for an hour or so.

Once the chocolate has hardened you can push it out of the mould. Serve the chocolate spoon on a saucer, next to a cup of hot milk. Stir to transform into the ultimate hot chocolate.

Chocolate melting tips Chocolate is delicate, and melting it is an art. It doesn't like getting wet, so make sure the bowl you use is absolutely dry. Here are the two most popular ways to melt.

Microwave Break the chocolate up into small chunks and put it in a dry microwaveable bowl. Pop it in the microwave on a medium heat (usually about 600W) for 30 seconds. Then have a quick look. Pop it back in the microwave for another 30 seconds. Now it will probably look a bit melted. Give it a stir. Keep going until it looks about 70% melted. Then stir and the melted chocolate will melt the rest fairly quickly. I find 100g (3½ oz) of chocolate generally needs about 2 minutes in the microwave. You don't want to just blast it for 2 minutes though, as that will burn the chocolate.

On the hob/stovetop This is where a recipe book usually calls for a bain marie, but who has one? The DIY alternative is to part-fill a small saucepan full of water. Bring the water to the boil. Break the chocolate up into small pieces and put in a large shallow heatproof glass bowl, which you rest on the saucepan's rim. The idea is that the bowl doesn't touch the water. Let the water simmer gently, heating the chocolate as you stir, until it has melted.

A confession I don't have a microwave or a heatproof bowl the right size to rest on the rim of any of my saucepans, so I place my heatproof glass jug in a large saucepan of simmering water. I don't want the jug to rest on the base of the saucepan, as that is too hot and may scorch the chocolate, so I place a small upside-down saucer on the base. Probably chocolatiers are rolling their eyes, but it works for me.

celebrate

If there was ever a more ludicrously titled chapter, we'd like to know it, because, friends, we are going to be honest. Big birthday parties for small kids are hell on earth. Who knew two hours could crawl by so slowly? Forget children in their party outfits cutely doing the actions to games like 'Oranges and Lemons'. Think instead of Lord of the Flies with party bags.

In our experience young kids love inviting the whole class so this may be something you have to do once in your/their life. As they get older (and you get wiser and start to indoctrinate them), they'd rather do something with just a few friends. Either way you don't want to be preoccupied with finessing your homemade mayonnaise when you're looking after a group of kids. So our advice when it comes to the food is keep it simple. You may be spending more time than anticipated just ensuring the kids don't escape (an idea we hadn't even considered until it started to happen). You may spend another half an hour trying to extricate Herbie from the loo, after he has accidentally locked himself in. You could find yourself doing all manner of things, but one thing we guarantee you won't be doing is ensuring that children eat healthily.

With that (and your mental health) in mind, may we recommend you peruse our savoury suggestions? They can all be made the night before if you ignore the sandwiches. This will give you more time on the day to PANIC! Alternatively, if you are of a less histrionic frame of mind than we are, you could use this time to calmly remove the jelly mould from the Bunny in the Grass Jelly (see opposite) or add the finishing touches to the birthday cakes (see pages 172 and 174). What you shouldn't do is make a start on the Prosecco you bought for the other parents. Well, not before midday.

BUNNY *in the grass jelly*

This is not strictly a recipe; more a serving suggestion, but a good one which our children love. All you need is a rabbit-shaped jelly mould, two packets of jelly/fruit gelatin — one green and one other colour for the bunny — and some fondant flowers to decorate. It is almost too cute to eat.

Make the jelly up as per packet instructions. Pour the green jelly into a bowl and the other colour into the bunny mould. Put the jellies in the fridge until firm. Mash up the green jelly with a fork. Carefully remove the bunny from the mould and place in the centre of a plate. Surround the bunny with the mashed up green jelly. Decorate with flowers. There you have it – a rabbit you won't feel bad about eating. Well, maybe just a little bit.

To remove jelly from the mould If you want to ensure your bunny doesn't lose his sweet little cotton bobtail, or even more tragically, half his face, follow these simple tips. Get a large bowl of warm water. It needs to be bigger than the jelly mould. Carefully lower the jelly mould into the water for a few seconds, making sure not to submerge the jelly. Lift the mould out and put a slightly wet plate on top (this allows you to move the jelly easily if it is not in the right spot) before turning it upside down (or just to confuse you, the right way up). Let the mould sit for a few seconds (glass and ceramic ones will need very little time, plastic less, metal even less), giving it the odd encouraging squeeze or shake. The jelly should fall out. A word of caution – make sure the water in the bowl is not too hot and the mould is not left in the water for too long, otherwise the bunny will melt.

SAVOURY *party*

Children's parties can be challenging – a bit like entering Dante's inferno clad in a clown's outfit with nothing but a bag of ice cubes and a cocktail umbrella as protection.

We have been to that hell. It was a scary place and our main advice is to pay someone else to provide the entertainment. Once Claire didn't and we're not sure her husband has been the same since. Anyway, when it comes to food, the advice is keep it simple.

We feel that as this is a recipe book, we should encourage you to spend hours fiddling about in the kitchen but, as we all know, the savoury food at a party is just the hors d'oeuvres to the sweet stuff.

So give the children what they want, which is basically *sausages.* You can never do too many; they will eat whatever you make, but maybe factor 4–5 cocktail sausages or a couple of chipolatas each. If you really want to blow their minds, give them Pigs in Blankets. Super-easy and they will love you forever. Just take a bacon slice, cut it in half and wind it around your chipolata. Push a cocktail stick through it and put it in a preheated 180°C/350°F/gas mark 4 oven for 25 minutes, or until the sausage is cooked. Another item to inspire true love is the sausage rolls on page 119; just leave out the onion marmalade if you think it will be too rich.

If you are doing a smaller party, *frankfurters* are a good option. There are some really delicious and well-sourced ones available, which are quick and easy to prepare. Stick them in a bun with some ketchup, maybe some fried onions and you're done.

Sandwiches are obviously a good idea. To taste halfway decent they need to be done the morning of the party. Allow half a sandwich per child, and keep it really simple with cream cheese on white bread, crusts off. You could be cute and cut them into shapes using a cookie cutter, but that's an additional job to do when really you should be spending all your time PANICKING. You can buy crustless bread from the supermarket that will save you a job and cream cheese means you don't need to butter the sandwiches. Maybe cut some cucumber into crudités as an attempt to salve your conscience. Carrot sticks and hummus always go down well.

Another great option is *pizza.* No child doesn't like pizza! Keep it simple though, tomato and mozzarella is the limit. No vegetables and NO anchovies! That way everyone will like what they've got and you won't be finding bits of red pepper stuck on the underside of tables for months afterwards. Obviously don't make the pizza yourself. Buy the bases and then pop the toppings on. Tomato purée/paste is perfectly acceptable as the base sauce, then drop on some mozzarella and season with black pepper. (Oh go on then, buy the whole thing – we won't tell anyone.) Serve at room temperature.

Crisps/potato chips are obviously essential and any child who doesn't get them on their birthday is entirely within their rights to call a child helpline. Potato rings are de rigueur.

SWEET *party*

True story: we once went to a party for a 4-year-old, where there was no cake and no chocolate; just little bowls of grapes and boxes of raisins for dessert. Breaking the news to our children that this was a cake-free party felt like telling them Santa Claus did not exist. Child cruelty writ large! We can't tell you if the misguided parents revised their no-cake policy for their daughter's next birthday, because they emigrated soon after. Probably out of shame.

Children's parties should run along the same principles as grown-up ones. Guests get to eat and drink as much as they want and dance like no one's watching.

That said, to please other parents more than anything, as soon as the sandwiches and crisps are finished, put out little bowls of cut-up grapes and strawberries. You could – if you wanted to up the ante – make a fruit rainbow using equal amounts of strawberries, satsuma segments, pineapple chunks, blueberries and black and green grapes arranged by colour in a rainbow shape on a large chopping board. It looks very pretty. Although, admittedly, not for long.

If the kids think this is the only sweet thing they are getting, they will eat lots of fruit and it counters all those potato rings and mini-sausages. Well, slightly.

While they are munching/throwing fruit, get the birthday cake ready. Once the candles have been blown out, cut up the cake and hand it out as a pudding. This is so much better than the arduous task of slicing it and wrapping it to go in the party bags under pressure as everyone is leaving. If you're anything like us, you will discover it several days later, squashed at the bottom of a handbag, growing mould and moulting crumbs.

If it is a smaller party, Bunny in the Grass Jelly (page 167) is always loved. Count on getting about 12 small portions out of each bunny and make sure you remember to bring bowls and spoons if the party's not at home.

Age-appropriate number cookies, iced garishly and decorated liberally with sprinkles, are always popular. See the simple recipe on page 171.

Of course, our way of doing things is by no means prescriptive. Don't feel guilty about buying stuff. (Did you know most supermarkets sell bags of ready-made fairy cakes, waiting to be iced? Well, so we've heard …) The only other advice we have is to make sure home time coincides with the peak of their sugar rush and that you have something nice and cold and possibly alcoholic waiting for you when the last guest goes home. You'll need it.

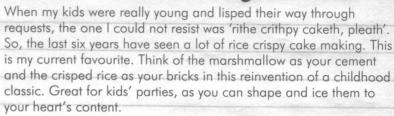

PIMPED-UP *rice crispy cakes*

45g (3 tbsp) butter
220g (8 oz) marshmallows
150g (6 cups) crisped rice cereal
30g (1 oz) chocolate, to decorate

Start to finish: 20 minutes prep
+ 30 minutes in the fridge

Makes: depending on the size of
your cutters, 6–8 cakes

When my kids were really young and lisped their way through requests, the one I could not resist was 'rithe crithpy caketh, pleath'. So, the last six years have seen a lot of rice crispy cake making. This is my current favourite. Think of the marshmallow as your cement and the crisped rice as your bricks in this reinvention of a childhood classic. Great for kids' parties, as you can shape and ice them to your heart's content.

Line a 20 x 30cm (8 x 12 inch) tray bake tin or any other dish that has a similar surface area with baking paper.

Put the butter into a medium-sized saucepan over a low heat. After a few seconds add the marshmallows. Really gently heat the mix until the marshmallows have lost their shape and you are left with a big goo. Take off the heat. If ever the mix looks like it's getting too hot and the marshmallow mix is going to burn, take it off the heat. The key is to do it slowly.

Once you have a marshmallow soup, stir in the crisped rice. Gently fold them in, making sure each one is coated. Empty the mixture into the lined tray bake tin.

Initially the mix will be too sticky to flatten. So wait for a couple of minutes, and then with clean hands press the mixture down. If the marshmallow is all stringy, then it's still too hot. Wait a bit longer. Then push down so it's all flat. Set aside to cool.

Flip the cake out of the tray. It should come out very easily still attached to the baking paper. Flip it over again so that the paper is on the bottom.

Using a cookie cutter, nothing too elaborate, hearts or circles are good, cut the crispy cake. Try not to eat too many offcuts …

Melt some chocolate (see page 164) and then drizzle over the cakes. Alternatively, partially dip them in melted chocolate for high impact.

Word to the wise Far be it from us to create gender-specific food. We just wanted to point out that a mixed bag of pink and white marshmallows will create very pink crispy rice cakes. If you think your 8-year-old son and all his mates will be happy with that, great! If not, maybe just stick to white marshmallows. And give them all pink balloons.

Claire

NUMBER *cookies*

150g (1 heaping cup) plain/
 all-purpose flour
50g (¼ cup) soft brown sugar
½ tsp baking powder
50g (scant ½ stick) butter, cubed
1 egg
30g (2 tbsp) runny honey

Icing
150g (1 cup) icing/confectioners'
 sugar
food colouring paste
lots of sprinkles

Start to finish: 20 minutes prep
+ 15 minutes baking

Makes: 10

Young children are very proud of getting older, so whilst these number biscuits work well for little ones, perhaps don't bake them for your mum. They should be garishly iced and covered in sprinkles.

Preheat the oven to 160°C/325°F/gas mark 3. Grease or line a large baking sheet.

Put the flour, sugar and baking powder into a food processor with the butter. Blitz it so it looks a bit like breadcrumbs. Then add the egg and honey. (This can be done by hand too, first of all using a spoon, then your hands.)

When you have a dough forming, stop the processor and take it out. If it's too sticky, add more flour. Flour the work surface and a rolling pin and roll out the dough so it is about 4mm (¼ inch) thick. Cut out with the cookie cutter and put the dough numbers spaced slightly apart onto the baking sheet as they spread a bit. Roll and recut the dough, until there is none left. Bake for about 15 minutes or until golden brown. Cool on a wire rack, ready for icing.

Sieve the icing/confectioners' sugar and mix with about a tablespoon of hot water. Add a tiny amount of food colouring and stir until the colour is even and there are no lumps in the icing (make sure it is not too runny or it will slide off). Spread over the cookies. While still wet, decorate with sprinkles. The best way to do this is to pour the sprinkles in a bowl and dip the cookie icing-side down into them. Allow to set. Pop them in the fridge if it is a warm day, to speed things up.

CHILDREN'S *party drinks*

In amongst all that piñata and popcorn it's easy to overlook drinks when it comes to kids' parties. But obviously they need to drink, as all that running around and creating mayhem is thirsty work. One suggestion is large jugs full of cordial or water and paper cups, but we advise caution as the spillage potential fills us with dread. And who's going to pour that big ol' jug? Fingers crossed it's you, but it might just be that weeny little 5-year-old over there. Ooops! Anyone got a cloth?

Far better are drinks in individual cartons with straws. Cartons of fruit juice are pretty cheap if you get them from a supermarket, and most parents won't object to their child being given fruit juice.

A great option is a small bottle of water with a sports cap, as the spillage potential is almost zero and it's healthy and economical. To avoid spending the party handing out bottles, because the child has put it down somewhere, put name labels on each bottle.

Drinks for grown-ups A request for a cup of tea is enough to send the host over the edge as it means locating kettle, cup, teabag, milk under layers of party food and napkins. If parents are staying (if your guests are under 5, they probably will), try having a bottle of Prosecco and fizzy water open, and some plastic cups (classy!). It's the easiest option and gives the party a little sparkle for adults. It might also stop them asking for that cup of tea.

BATTLE *of the birthday cakes: part 1*

INGREDIENTS

100g (3½ oz) dark/semisweet
  chocolate (70% cocoa)
150ml (⅔ cup) milk
225g (1¾ cups) self-raising flour
2 tbsp cocoa powder
2 tsp baking powder
225g (2 sticks) butter, at room
  temperature
225g (1 heaping cup) caster/
  superfine sugar
4 eggs, beaten

Filling, icing and decorations
3 tbsp raspberry jam
100g (3½ oz) dark/semisweet
  chocolate (70% cocoa)
50g (scant ½ stick) butter
50g (heaping ⅓ cup) icing/
  confectioners' sugar
250g (9 oz) milk chocolate fingers
ribbon, to decorate
fresh raspberries, strawberries or
  other decorations (see photo)

Start to finish: 15 minutes prep
+ 45 minutes in the oven + icing

Serves: 10

Big and small This cake will take
40–45 minutes to bake. If you just
bake one large cake and slice it in
half horizontally it will take about
60 minutes, but it will be slightly
drier (not a huge issue once it has
been smothered in chocolate icing
and raspberry jam, so fine if you
only have one deep cake tin).
Alternatively make the cake batter
and bake in individual fairy cake
cases, checking for doneness after
about 15–20 minutes.

Claire's cake: I love a fairy princess castle cake as much as the next
person. I am constantly amazed by Lucy's creations (see overleaf).
I like to ooh! and ahh! over her imaginative use of doilies, the
mechanics of the chocolate finger drawbridge, the expressive use
of sprinkles. But do I want to eat it? Um, probably not. I know that's
not the point. I know it's theme cakes that little girls' and little boys'
dreams are made of, but I can't quite make myself spend the required
time and energy on something I won't eat.

So I always go for plan B. And plan B is chocolate, so as plan Bs go,
it's not bad. Make a big chocolate cake and then smother in more
chocolate. Line the outside of the cake with chocolate fingers and fill
the middle with fruit or your child's favourite sweets, depending on
how kind you are feeling.

Preheat the oven to 180°C/350°F/gas mark 4. Line and butter two
20cm (8 inch) cake pans.

Put the chocolate in a small saucepan with the milk. Heat the
milk and let the chocolate slowly melt, then let it cool.

Put the flour, cocoa powder and baking powder into a large bowl.
Give it a good stir. Add the butter, sugar, beaten eggs and
chocolate milk.

Using an electric whisk, beat until it is well combined and pale.
Divide evenly into the two prepared cake tins and place in the
oven. Check the cakes after about 40 minutes. It is quite a
mousse-y cake, so the top might not spring back when it's
cooked. Don't worry, it's ready when you stick a knife or skewer
in the centre of the cake and it comes out clean.

Once the cakes have cooled slightly, turn them out onto a wire
rack to completely cool.

When cool, choose the least attractive cake for the base and put
it on the serving plate. Spread the top with raspberry jam and
place the second cake on top, making sure the smoothest, most
attractive surface is at the top.

To make the icing, melt the chocolate (see page 164), then stir in
the butter and icing/confectioners' sugar. Keep stirring until it's
completely mixed together. Spread over the top of the cake, and
down the sides. It may not reach all the way down, but that's fine.

Once iced (which is easier than it sounds), place a single layer of
chocolate fingers around the outside. The bottom of each finger
should touch the plate. When you've finished, use a ribbon to tie
around the outside of the cake to secure the fingers. Then scatter
the top with raspberries, halved strawberries, chocolate buttons,
gummy bears, or anything else your child requests.

Tricks and treats Other tricks when it comes to birthday cakes include using the same cake batter to make smaller fairy cakes to ice with chocolate and decorate. Pop them on a tiered cake stand, add some candles and serve.

BATTLE *of the birthday cakes: part 2*

Cake
2 batches of Victorian Mess
  sponge cake batter (see
  page 183)
8 tbsp raspberry jam
2 shop-bought Madeira/pound
  loaf cakes (300g/10½ oz
  each). Of course you can
  make your own if you prefer!

Buttercream icing
500g (4½ sticks) unsalted butter
  at room temperature (see tip
  page 183)
1kg (2¼ lb) icing/confectioners'
  sugar
food colouring paste (optional)

Ice cream cone towers
200g (7 oz) white chocolate,
  4 ice cream cones and
  candy sprinkles
or 4 paper doilies

Decorations
red liquorice strips
jelly diamonds
silver balls
mini marshmallows
mini princess/prince figures
  (optional)

Equipment
2 x 20cm (8 inch) square cake tins
30cm (12 inch) square cake board
  covered in foil or wrapping
  paper

Start to finish: 20 minutes to
make the sponges, 40 minutes
to bake them, a couple of hours
cooling time, 30 minutes to make
the icing and decorate.

Makes: 16–24 slices depending
on slice size

Lucy's cake: For my sixth birthday, our mum baked a fairy castle cake. Pale pink with turrets topped with paper doilies, marshmallow steps up which ballerinas danced to a door made from silver sprinkles. It was the best cake in the world and Mum still has the photo of me standing in front of it, jaw dropped, looking as if I had won the lottery. When my daughters saw the picture, they asked for this cake for their birthdays, and now in generational symmetry we have pictures of them looking as awestruck as I did all those years ago.

Preheat the oven to 190°C/375°F/gas mark 5.

Using the recipe on page 183, make 2 batches of the Victorian Mess cake batter. Divide the mixture between 2 greased and lined 20cm (8 inch) square cake tins. Bake for 40 minutes. Cool on a wire rack.

For the icing, cream the butter and icing/confectioners' sugar together with a hand-held electric whisk until soft. Mix in tiny amounts of food colouring until you get the desired colour.

When the cakes are cool, place the worst-looking Victoria sponge dome-side down (the weight will flatten it out) on the cake board. Spread 7 tbsp jam on top and then place the other sponge dome-side down on top of the jam. This leaves you with your best and flattest surface to ice.

Cut the Madeira/pound loaf cakes in half, forming 4 square tower-shaped pieces. Using the remaining jam as glue, stick a tower onto each corner of your sponge cakes. The towers should all be the same height, so use a ruler.

For the turrets, either fashion cones out of paper doilies or cover 4 ice-cream cones in melted chocolate and sprinkles. The best way is to put a wooden spoon handle inside a cone, holding it over a bowl of melted white chocolate (break chocolate up and zap it in the microwave on medium in 30 second bursts until melted, stirring occasionally). Spoon it over the cone until covered. Then, hold the cone over a plate and pour on the sprinkles. This has to be done when the chocolate is still wet, otherwise they won't stick. Stand the cones on a plate, leave them to dry in the fridge and get on with the business of icing.

Ice the cake on the board it will be served on, as this means you won't have the heart-stopping process of transferring it from a plate to the board later. Put a big dollop of icing on the cake and spread it over, working out from the middle to the sides. Use a palette knife or, if you don't have one, a (clean) credit card or ruler will be admirable substitutes. Put a bit on all the sides and the towers and spread. Try not to get crumbs in the icing. Professionals make double the amount of icing and do a first crumb layer, then chill for 2 hours before doing a second perfect layer. We don't think anyone minds a few crumbs, and if they do, it says more about them than it does about your baking skills.

Then the fun begins... Once the chocolate on the cones has set, add the turrets. Get your red liquorice strips, jelly diamonds, silver balls and mini marshmallows ready and decorate as you wish. This is a cake that cannot be overdone. Mini princesses or princes stationed around the palace always go down well.

PS This cake can very easily be turned into a chocolate fort. Just make a chocolate sponge instead (for every 100g/¾ cup flour, substitute 25g/3 tbsp flour for 25g/3 tbsp cocoa) and chocolate buttercream icing. Decorate with chocolate buttons and chocolate fingers. I did this one year as Hogwarts, Harry Potter's school.

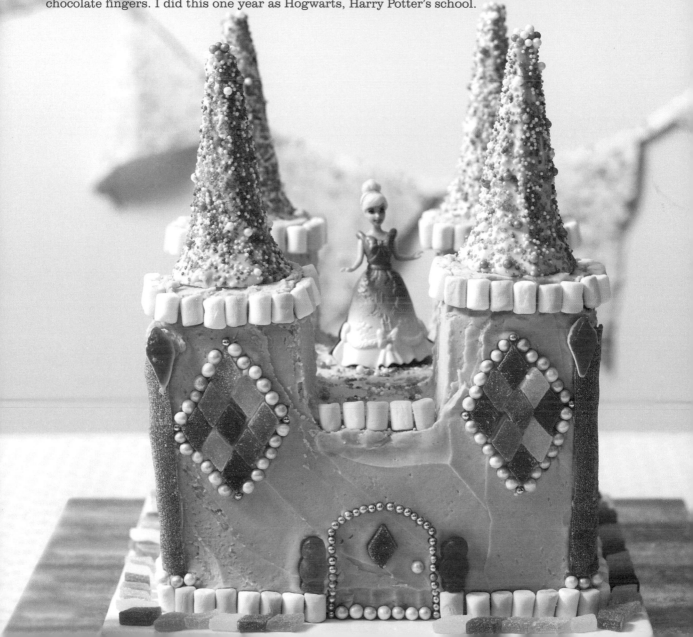

baking

We love to bake. It is magic – just by mixing a few ingredients, stirring and baking, something heavenly emerges.

Baking can be daunting as it is one area of cooking where precision matters. But it's not rocket science – if you get the quantities wrong or forget to set the timer, the worst that will happen is your cake turns out a bit flat or slightly burnt. No one will really mind though, they will just be pleased you made the effort. Hopefully.

There are a few simple tips that make mistakes less likely. Invest in good scales. We like digital ones that also measure liquids. Eggs and butter should be at room temperature (see our tip for softening butter on page 183, and no, it doesn't include shoving it down your bra). Baking powder (and indeed self-raising flour) must be fresh to ensure sponges rise. Cake tins should be greased and ovens preheated. Incidentally, ovens all vary, so get to know yours and how quickly it cooks. There are still corners to be cut, like sieving. We never bother and haven't noticed the difference. Our cakes still rise beautifully. The exception is icing sugar. If you don't sieve it, your icing will resemble pebbledash.

So these are the tips, now for the recipes. If you need something in a hurry, we are proud of our three-ingredient peanut butter cookies on page 187. Our eight-apple cake on page 178 has so much fruit in it, it is practically a health food. There are cakes for every eventuality. If Armageddon strikes, our long-lasting banana bread baked in a jar on page 185 (CAKE! IN A JAR!) could see you through. Don't mock, it could save your life.

SAINT/SINNER *fruit loaf*

500g (3¾ cups) mixed dried fruit
300ml (1¼ cups) black tea
250g (scant 2 cups) self-raising flour
50g (½ cup) ground almonds
(optional; if not using, increase
the flour by this amount)
125g (⅔ cup) dark brown sugar
1 heaped tsp mixed spice (or a
combination of cinnamon,
nutmeg, ginger, whatever you
have in your cupboard)
2 eggs
10–12 glacé/candied cherries
20 whole unblanched almonds

Start to finish: 24 hours soaking,
10 minutes prep + up to 1½ hours
in the oven

Serves: 10

By day this is a glorious fruit cake, studded with almonds and cherries. Great with a cup of tea, you could serve it to your granny. By night it's a different affair altogether. Perhaps it's that dusky sky or the candlelight, but suddenly the cherries glint seductively. Bring out the port and serve with cheese for a far more grown-up experience.

Place the mixed dried fruit and the black tea in a large bowl, cover with a plate and leave to soak for 24 hours.

When you are ready to make your cake, preheat the oven to 180°C/350°F/gas mark 4. Line a 900g (9 x 5 x 2 inch) loaf tin with baking paper or use a pre-pleated paper liner if you have one.

To the fruit and tea mixture, add the flour, ground almonds, sugar, mixed spice and eggs. Stir, so that all the ingredients are fully mixed.

Pour the mixture into the loaf tin. Sprinkle the top with the glacé cherries and whole almonds. Bake for 1 hour, then check to see if it is done by inserting a thin skewer into the centre. It should come out clean. If not, return to the oven. Unlike a sponge, it won't quickly burn, so check again in 5–10 minutes.

Allow it to cool thoroughly on a wire rack, then firmly wrap in foil. It will last for up to three weeks.

Saint or sinner? If you would rather your fruit cake was more sinner than saint, you can dowse it with brandy. When it is about two days old, prick the surface all over with a skewer and brush with 2 tbsp brandy.

Serve with... If the cake turns out dark and dense, serve it with Stilton. If softer, go for something a touch lighter, such as Roquefort.

EIGHT-APPLE cake

8 small eating apples, peeled, cored
    and chopped (you need about
    450g/1 lb of apples)
juice of 1 lemon
½ tsp ground cinnamon
200g (1½ cups) plain/all-purpose
    flour
1½ tsp baking powder
200g (1 cup) caster/superfine sugar
3 eggs
6 level tbsp melted butter
1–2 tbsp milk, as needed
1 tbsp demerara/light brown sugar,
    for topping

Start to finish: 10 minutes prep
+ 50 minutes in the oven

Makes: 8–10 slices

This is an apple cake like no other and one of my favourite puddings, lunches, breakfasts or afternoon snacks ever. It is delicious with a double espresso as an early morning perk-me-up, with a hunk of strong cheese at lunchtime or on its own anytime. It is foolproof to make; the only fiddle is the peeling.

Preheat the oven to 180°C/350°F/gas mark 4. Grease and line a 20cm (8 inch) round springform cake tin or an 18cm (7 inch) square cake tin.

Toss the apples in the lemon juice and ground cinnamon the minute they're chopped to stop them going brown.

Combine the flour, baking powder and sugar in a separate bowl. Add the eggs and butter and beat with a wooden spoon to make a stiff batter. Add milk if it seems a bit dry. Fold the apples (and any remaining lemon juice) into the batter. Pour into the cake tin, smooth down and sprinkle with demerara/light brown sugar.

Bake for 45–50 minutes or until a skewer comes out clean. Allow to cool slightly, then turn out onto a wire rack.

Get creative Substitute half the butter with mild olive oil, add some chopped walnuts and it's the perfect accompaniment for cheese. I have successfully substituted a handful of ground almonds for a handful of flour, olive oil for the butter and milk for plain/natural yogurt and although slightly different each time, it is always delicious.

Lucy

BANANA AND HONEY
oat cookies

These are a brilliant after-school snack. The promise of freshly baked banana cookies puts an end to the constant requests for chocolate bars and ice cream on their way home. The kids needn't know they took minutes to prepare and have no sugar in them, just banana and honey.

Preheat the oven to 180°C/350°F/gas mark 4. Line a baking sheet with baking paper.

In a bowl, using a blender, blitz the bananas, oats, baking powder and salt. Add the melted butter, honey and egg and stir. Once it's all mixed, stir in the chocolate chips, if you are feeling kind.

With a teaspoon, scoop out a blob of the mixture and place it on the baking sheet. This recipe makes about 18 small cookies, so lay them out on the sheet with space between them to allow them to spread. Put them in the middle of the oven, and bake for about 15–20 minutes, until they are golden brown.

If you manage to get the kids home before you dish them up, rather than eating on the hoof during the school run, serve alongside a small cup of milk.

INGREDIENTS

2 small ripe bananas
   (approx 200g/7 oz)
200g (2 heaping cups) porridge/
   rolled oats
1 tsp baking powder
pinch of salt
75g (5 tbsp) butter, melted
2 tsp honey
1 egg, beaten
handful of chocolate chips
   (optional)

Start to finish: 10 minutes prep + 20 minutes in the oven

Makes: 18

Claire

GINGERBREAD

INGREDIENTS

300g (2¼ cups) plain/all-purpose flour
1½ tsp ground ginger
½ tsp ground cinnamon
1 tsp bicarbonate of soda/baking soda
125g (1 stick) unsalted butter, plus extra for greasing, at room temperature
100g (½ cup) soft brown sugar – muscovado/dark brown molasses sugar is nice, but whatever you have is fine
3½ tbsp golden syrup/light corn syrup
1 egg, beaten

Icing
50g (heaping ⅓ cup) icing/confectioners' sugar
few drops of water
raisins and sprinkles

Start to finish: 10 minutes + however long the kids take to cut them out + 15 minutes in the oven

Makes: 20 big cookies

Did you know that perfect parenthood is just 10 minutes away? You can have a house filled with the aroma of baking gingerbread, children whose artistic urges have been sated (momentarily) with a cookie cutter, and all the power of a parent wielding sweet things for the rest of the day. Yep, it's this simple.

Preheat the oven to 180°C/350°F/gas mark 4. Line two baking sheets with baking paper. Use a bit of butter on the underside to stop the paper from flapping up.

Put the flour, ginger, cinnamon and bicarbonate of soda/baking soda in a bowl and mix until mixed evenly.

Take the butter and use your fingertips to rub it into the flour mixture until it looks like breadcrumbs. Or use your food processor. Then sprinkle in the sugar and make sure it is mixed evenly. Using your hands is easiest for this too.

Add the golden syrup/light corn syrup (see below) and egg, and stir until most of the gloopy stuff is combined. Then I use my hands again to push the mixture together into one big ball of dough.

Roll the dough out on a floured surface until about 5mm (¼ inch) thick and cut out shapes using cookie cutters. Place them on the prepared baking sheets.

Put in the oven and bake until they are golden brown, which should take between 10–15 minutes depending on your oven. Let them cool on the baking sheet for a few minutes, and then place them on a wire rack to finish cooling. Make up the icing (see below) and decorate with an array of raisins and sprinkles.

Measuring golden syrup
It is a well-known fact that it's possible to use every spoon in the house when it comes to measuring golden syrup. But fear not, we have the answer (if you have digital scales). Pop the ingredients bowl on the scales and pour in the golden syrup. Most digital scales will measure ml/fl oz so measure out 15ml per tablespoon needed. This way you can do it accurately while just using one tablespoon. Another method is to grease a tablespoon with butter and pour the syrup into the spoon. The syrup will simply slide off the spoon when you add it to the other ingredients.

Icing Add the water to the icing sugar very slowly. You don't want a runny solution; it needs to be really sticky as it will act like glue to stick the decorations to the gingerbread. Mix it in a small cup and use the handle end of a teaspoon to apply it.

Freezing This freezes like a dream. Just roll the dough into a ball, wrap in clingfilm/plastic wrap and pop in the freezer. At the risk of sounding perfect (ha ha HA!) We always have a bit of this in the freezer. It defrosts quickly, and is brilliant when you've got half an hour to kill, or a rainy afternoon. Kids never seem to get bored with it.

170g (1¼ cups) self-raising flour
170g (heaping ¾ cup) caster/
   superfine sugar
170g (1½ sticks) unsalted butter,
   room temperature
1 tsp baking powder
1 tsp vanilla extract
3 eggs

Topping
2 tbsp raspberry jam
300ml (1¼ cups) double/heavy
   cream
big handful of fresh or frozen
   raspberries
25g (1 oz) meringue

Start to finish: 20 minutes prep
+ 25 minutes in the oven

Serves: depends on greed!
Perhaps 10

Eat me quick! You need to eat this quickly. Yep, all of it! The meringue won't stay crunchy in the cream for long, so it's a good idea to make the topping just before you serve – although a sprinkling of meringue on the top at the last minute will overcome this. And cream doesn't hang around, so eat it a day or so after making, and keep it in the fridge.

Warm me up! Dang! The butter is rock solid, but you need to make that cake NOW. Body heat isn't the answer, so take it out of your bra and instead run some hot water into a small bowl. Submerge the butter in it, count to five and remove it. Ta da! Perfect soft butter.

VICTORIAN mess

Has having kids meant you've stopped getting the attention you used to? Do the sleepless nights and constant tantrums mean your sparkling wit has dulled, your good looks faded? Fear not. This cake will rectify all that. Enter a room with this show-stopping combination of Victoria sponge and Eton Mess, and you will be the centre of all conversation. Conversation that will probably start with 'Can I have some cake please?'

Preheat the oven to 180°C/350°F/gas mark 4. Line the base and lightly butter the sides of two 20cm (8 inch) round cake tins.

Place all the cake ingredients in a large bowl. With an electric whisk (or a wooden spoon and a very strong arm), combine them all for about a minute until well mixed to a light, airy batter. The mix should slip off the spoon/mixer. If not, add a splash of milk to loosen.

Pour the batter into the cake tins, using a spatula to get the last bit out, and even the top. Put in the middle of a fan oven, or the top of a conventional one, for 25 minutes. Once baked, the top of the cake should spring back when lightly pressed, and a skewer should come out clean.

Let it cool slightly and then loosen the cakes from the sides of the tins with a knife. Turn onto a wire rack and let cool.

Once the cakes have cooled, use the least attractive cake as the base and cover its top with jam. Place the other cake on top.

When you are ready to ice the cake, whip the cream in a large bowl with an electric whisk. Once thickened, throw in the berries and stir them in, crushing some with a wooden spoon so the cream changes colour and becomes marbled with juice. Then crumble in most of the meringue and gently stir in.

Spread the cream/berry mix evenly over the top of the cake. Crumble the remaining meringue on top. Stand back. Admire.

300g (10½ oz) ginger nut biscuits/
  gingersnaps
110g (1 stick) unsalted butter,
  melted
600g (21 oz) full-fat cream cheese
225g (1 heaping cup) caster/
  superfine sugar
150g (⅔ cup) plain yogurt
2 large eggs
finely grated zest of 2 unwaxed
  lemons
juice of 1 lemon
50g (heaping ⅓ cup) plain/
  all-purpose flour
200g (7 oz) fresh raspberries
3 tbsp Lemon Curd (see page 140)

Start to finish: 15 minutes prep
+ 45 minutes in the oven
+ 1 hour cooling time

Serves 6–8

Lucy

LEMON CURD
and raspberry cheesecake

This is a showstopper of a dessert and as all the hard work can be done the night before, it is perfect for impressing friends at lunch or dinner.

Preheat the oven to 120°C/250°F/gas mark ½ and line the base of a 20cm (8 inch) round springform cake tin.

Put the biscuits in a carefully sealed plastic bag and work out some aggression by using a rolling pin to bash them up. If you don't feel the need to let off steam, use a food processor. You want fine-ish crumbs.

Put them in a large bowl with the melted butter and mix well. Push the mixture into an even layer in the base of the cake tin and chill. The biscuits, not you!

In a clean bowl, whisk (electric, if you have one) the cream cheese and sugar until well mixed. Beat in the yogurt and the eggs, lemon zest, juice and flour with a wooden spoon. Carefully fold through most of the raspberries (the rest are for decoration) and 2 tablespoons of the lemon curd. Take the tin from the fridge and place it on a baking sheet. Carefully pile the lemony cheese mixture on top of the biscuit base and smooth over.

Bake for 1 hour or until completely set. To check poke it – gently – in the middle; it should bounce back. Leave the cake in the oven to cool for a further hour or so, otherwise it will crack when you take it out.

Decorate with the remaining raspberries and drizzle with the remaining lemon curd (if you heat it gently it will be easier to drizzle). Wait for the applause. Curtsey!

Note You can use a combination of blueberries and raspberries, too.

BANANA BREAD
in a jar

INGREDIENTS

2 ripe bananas
110g (1 stick) butter
150g (¾ cup) caster/superfine sugar
2 eggs
225g (1¾ cups) self-raising flour
40g (¼ cup) chocolate chips
(broken- up chocolate, leftover
chocolate decorations) or
chopped unsalted nuts of your
choice

Start to finish: 10 minutes prep
+ 35–50 minutes in the oven

Makes: 6 jars or 1 loaf

The jars You need completely straight-sided jars as otherwise the cake won't slide out at the end (that is, unless you want to eat it straight from the jar). This is harder than it sounds, but straight-sided jars can be found online or Bonne Maman jam jars work well. Most jam jars are OK to cook on a low heat.

Sometimes it is fun to do something just because you can. This banana bread, baked in a jam jar, is a case in point. It is cake! In a jar! You can eat it with a spoon! Apparently, if the jars are sterilised (see page 163) it stays fresh up to six months, although it has never lasted more than a week in our homes. It is good for packed lunches, camping trips and forthcoming zombie invasions. The more conventional/sane amongst you can cook this banana bread as normal in a 900g (9 x 5 inch) loaf tin.

Preheat the oven to 140°C/275°F/gas mark 1.

Mash the bananas. Cream the butter and sugar together until a pale cream colour and fluffy. Save your muscles and use a hand-held mixer for this. Add the eggs. Stir in the flour. Mix everything together. Fold in the chocolate chips or nuts.

Divide the mixture between 6 sterilised jars (see page 163). They need to be filled just over a third full. Make sure there is no mixture spilled on the sides. Place on a baking sheet and bake for about 35–40 minutes. They will be done when they have risen to just below the top and when an inserted skewer comes out clean. Cool slightly and screw the lid on.

If you are using a loaf tin, bake for about 50 minutes at 180°C/350°F/gas mark 4.

SIMPLE *soda bread*

2 tbsp lemon juice
340ml (1½ cups) milk
500g (3¾ cups) plain/all-purpose
    flour
1 tsp bicarbonate of soda/baking
    soda
1 tsp salt

Start to finish: 10 minutes
+ 45 minutes in the oven

Makes: 1 large loaf

DIY buttermilk Lots of soda bread recipes call for buttermilk. It reacts with the bicarbonate of soda to make the bread rise.

It is readily available from most supermarkets nowadays but, unless you are very well prepared, it's unlikely you will always have it in your fridge. The milk/lemon juice trick lets you make soda bread spontaneously, whenever you fancy.

Another alternative to buttermilk is live full-fat yogurt.

You're that parent at the school gate with a beatific smile, a faraway look in your eyes, and maybe a picturesque dab of flour on your cheek. Why? Because you bake your own bread. When you are not cycling to school (your bike has a basket, obviously), you skip. OK, so all the other parents hate you and your smug freshly-baked smell. What they don't realise is that the bread you make is soda bread, so easy, but so delicious. No yeast, no waiting around, just a bit of mixing and then stick it in the oven. Bam! Halo.

Preheat the oven to 200°C/400°F/gas mark 6.

Stir the lemon juice into the milk and leave for 5 minutes. During this time the milk will curdle – don't worry! This is an essential part of the process (see left).

Put the flour, bicarbonate of soda/baking soda and salt in a large bowl and give it a good stir so the ingredients are well mixed. Add the milk/lemon mix and stir with a fork. This isn't a normal type of bread dough; aim for something a little drier than cake batter. If it feels too dry, add a splash more milk; if too wet, a little more flour, or a handful of oats works really well too.

This mix is difficult to knead; instead use a metal spoon or fork to bring it together into a ball in the bowl. Turn it out onto a baking paper-lined baking sheet. If that turns it into too much of a splodge, use a spoon to tidy it a bit. Then, using a serrated knife, cut a cross in the top of the bread (rumoured to let the devil out while it's cooking!) and give it a dusting of flour.

Put it in the oven for 45 minutes. To check it's done, use a clean tea/dish towel to take it out of the oven and give it a knock underneath. It should sound hollow. Not a bit hollow or hollow-ish, that means it is only part cooked, but properly hollow, so if needs be, stick it back in the oven for a few more minutes.

Serve immediately, warm with salted butter. Maybe some soup on the side, but then again, maybe not. Maybe just a whole loaf of bread, right now, for lunch, as it tastes much better on the day it is baked.

THREE-INGREDIENT
peanut butter cookies

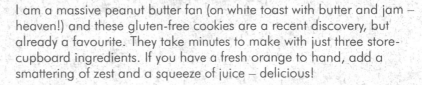

INGREDIENTS

115g (½ cup) peanut butter
100g (½ cup) brown sugar
1 egg
zest and juice of 1 orange (optional)

Start to finish: 2 minutes prep
+ 12 minutes baking

Makes: 10–12

I am a massive peanut butter fan (on white toast with butter and jam – heaven!) and these gluten-free cookies are a recent discovery, but already a favourite. They take minutes to make with just three store-cupboard ingredients. If you have a fresh orange to hand, add a smattering of zest and a squeeze of juice – delicious!

Preheat the oven to 180°C/350°F/gas mark 4.

Put the ingredients in a bowl and mix together. Add orange zest and juice if using – only a couple of grates of zest and a tiny splash of orange juice.

Use a teaspoon to measure out each cookie on a lined baking sheet. They spread while cooking, so space them about 2cm (¾ inch) apart. Don't worry if they are a bit higgledy-piggledy. Use a fork to flatten them (this will ensure they bake evenly too). Bake for 10–12 minutes until lightly browned.

Transfer to a wire rack and cool. They are best eaten on the day.

Pick of the pops Peanut butter is the perfect store-cupboard staple. Not only is it great for baking, but it works in savoury dishes too. Mix 3 tbsp peanut butter with 3 tbsp sweet chilli sauce, 2 tbsp soy sauce and 100ml (scant ½ cup) water for an accompaniment to chicken satay, or mix it with some garlic, oil and soy sauce for a chicken marinade (See Mild Mango Chicken Curry on page 36).

Lucy

INDEX

Acknowledgments

Claire: To my dearest husband, Liam, you are the air in my soufflé, the 70% cocoa chocolate in my brownies, the truffle on my pasta. Thank you for your help in writing this book, and your help in creating the family which inspired it.

Rufus, Bruno, what can I say? Thank you for your adventurous taste buds, your willingness to try anything (except green stuff) and your refreshing honesty when it comes to letting me know exactly what you don't like about each dish. Even at the ages of four and six, I see great futures ahead of you both as food critics.

Thanks also to all our friends and family whose wonderful recipes I've stolen for the book. Brendan, thanks for caring for the children so brilliantly and the alacrity (yes! alacrity!) with which you helped create some of these recipes. Tristan, thanks for your delicious curry. Joy, your fruit cake is second to none, it lives on in this book as Saint/Sinner Fruit Loaf. Thank you Agni, for your great Cypriot suggestions, many of which I've included, and have become firm favourites in our household. Carolina, thanks for your tips and help with some of the recipes, it is much appreciated.

And to my dear sister. My hope is that my two get on as well as we do. It makes the world a better place.

Lucy: Julia Child said people who love to eat are always the best people and James, you are the best of them all. Thanks for coming on this and every other adventure with me, for making the best sandwiches in London, but most of all for cutting your onions so small.

To my two bobby dazzlers, Elizabeth and Sophia. I am never happier than when sat at the kitchen table with you. As testament to your brilliance, all the broccoli recipes in this book are dedicated to you both. Big love.

To Claire, if I didn't have a sister, I would make one up just like you.

Thanks to all my friends and family whose recipes feature in this book. John and Lauren Goldsmith for their Greenwich Bake, Andreas of Chelsea for introducing me to cavolo nero, Chiswick's Grove Park Deli for their sausage and onion marmalade rolls, Mum for her legendary chocolate fudge pudding, Aunty Margaret for butter-making, Vic O'Bree for her sizzling chorizo and prawns, Holly Graham for loving my Eight Apple Cake so much, she made her own version and to Serena Mackesy for the drinks inspiration.

To Professor Tim Lang at City University for helping me see what I eat in a different way and to all the other food campaigners out there continuing the good fight.

Claire & Lucy: To Elly James at HHB – you are one in a million. At Cico Books thanks to Mark McGinlay for taking us with you, to Gillian Haslam for your patience, to Sally Powell and to Cindy Richards for having faith in us. To Hannah George for the brilliant cartoons, and to Stuart West, Emily Jonzen, Luis Peral Ananda and Mark Latter for making the food look so nice.

To Andy Taylor, Selma Turajlic and Holly Graham at Little Dot for their help, guidance and knowledge in this brave new world.

But most of all thanks to the kindred spirits we have met en route our culinary journey – the food bloggers, YouTubers, readers and parents helping make the world a better place one meal at a time. Peace, love and broccoli pasta.